Ex-Etiquette

for

Weddings

The Blended Families' Guide to Tying the Knot

Jann Blackstone-Ford and Sharyl Jupe

CHICAGO
REVIEW
PRESS

Library of Congress Cataloging-in-Publication Data
Blackstone-Ford, Jann.
    Ex-etiquette for weddings : the blended families' guide to tying the knot /
Jann Blackstone-Ford and Sharyl Jupe.—1st ed.
    p. cm.
    Includes bibliographical references and index.
    ISBN-13: 978-1-55652-671-8
    ISBN-10: 1-55652-671-7
1. Weddings—Planning. 2. Wedding etiquette. 3. Remarriage.
4. Stepfamilies. I. Jupe, Sharyl. II. Title.

    HQ745.B63 2007
    395.2'2—dc22

Cover and interior design: Scott Rattray
Cover photo: Neo Vision
Author photo: Larry Ford

© 2007 by Jann Blackstone-Ford, M.A.
All rights reserved
First edition
Published by Chicago Review Press, Incorporated
814 North Franklin Street
Chicago, Illinois 60610
ISBN-13: 978-1-55652-671-8
ISBN-10: 1-555652-671-7
Printed in the United States of America
5 4 3 2 1

Contents

ACKNOWLEDGMENTS iv
INTRODUCTION vi

1. Laying the Groundwork 1

2. Your Engagement 20

3. Setting the Budget 39

4. Getting Organized 51

5. Attendants and Attire 72

6. Guest List and Invitations 88

7. Showers and Bachelor and
Bachelorette Parties 117

8. The Rehearsal Dinner 130

9. The Ceremony 134

10. The Reception 157

11. Destination and Theme Weddings,
Honeymoons, and Familymoons 177

12. Formalities 186

RESOURCES 199
BIBLIOGRAPHY 209
INDEX 210

Acknowledgments

It's always difficult for Sharyl and me to express how grateful we are for the support we receive when writing an ex-etiquette book, but we will try to list everyone who helped us make *Ex-Etiquette for Weddings* a reality.

First, thank you to our family for supporting our passion for getting the word out about good ex-etiquette. Mel, Anee, Steven, Harleigh, and, of course, Larry have been both a part of combined family living and witnesses to its growing pains, and they've worked to change the way society views life after divorce or separation. It's important that we start by saying how much we love them and value their support in all this.

We would also like to thank Michael Mew and Jennifer Bain (Anee's father and her father's wife) for being of inspiration during this writing, and all the members of the Bonus Families organization whose donations have enabled us to give back something of importance.

Thanks to Dr. Susan Bartell for her support and friendship. To Cynthia Sherry and Lisa Reardon from Chicago Review Press for their patience and excellent ideas for editing these projects—what a joy to find a publisher who is so easy to work with! And to Sara Hoerdeman, our cheerleader and new friend—who is possibly the best publicity manager in the entire world—and the entire publicity team at Chicago

Review Press, especially Elizabeth Malzahn, who works so hard to support us whenever we need it. You guys are the best!

Our thanks to our wonderful literary agent, Djana Pearson Morris, for her understanding, support, and enthusiasm; she has been with us from the beginning and does a great job of keeping us focused. And to everyone who uses the term *bonus*—positive change always starts with changing ourselves first.

Introduction

In 1989 I married Larry Ford, the ex-husband of my coauthor, Sharyl Jupe. She became my nemesis, and I hers. Sharyl and Larry had joint physical custody of their two children. Steven was four and Melanie had just turned eight. I had a child, Anee, who was seven, from a previous marriage. Larry and Sharyl could not talk to each other productively or civilly, yet the kids were going back and forth, a week at a time, between Sharyl's home and our home. (My ex-husband and I weren't on the best terms either. Even though we had joint custody of Anee, I retained sole physical custody; therefore, we had a more conventional divorced relationship. He lived an hour away and we rarely talked—even though we should have.) Sharyl hated the lack of control she had over her children when they were in my home, which translated into her hating me. On the other side, because Sharyl's kids spent so much time at my house, every rule that Sharyl set for her children affected my child. That translated into my not liking Sharyl much either.

Unfortunately, no one told any of us that we were doing it wrong. We thought we were doing it the way you had to if you were divorced. Divorced parents don't like each other. Divorced parents fight. That's the way it is. But when the children began to display problems that we attributed to the stress in the homes—one child had chronic stomachaches and another had trouble sleeping—that's when all the adults knew we had to find a better way.

Sharyl and I eventually called a truce for the sake of the kids. It wasn't a formal truce, where one of us suddenly waved a white flag and ended the war. It was a gradual acceptance of each other's role in respect to the children in our care. We began to cooperate with each other—and surprisingly, as we cooperated with each other, Larry and Sharyl began to work through their differences too. Sharyl and I now regard each other as close friends. It was a logical progression—we both love the same kids.

Somewhere in the midst of all these trials and tribulations, I went back to college. My chosen profession was mediation, and I learned to apply the tricks of that trade to my life. My specialty became divorce, child custody, and visitation. In 2000 I started the nonprofit organization Bonus Families to help divorced parents and bonusfamily members navigate the treacherous waters of divorce and remarriage. We offer workshops, mediation, support groups, and advice to divorced parents and bonusfamilies. Sharyl was instrumental in the formation and serves on the board of directors. We were living the organization's goals.

Out of Bonus Families grew our first book, *Ex-Etiquette for Parents: Good Behavior After a Divorce or Separation*. It established a model for more positive communication between divorced or separated parents. We chose *Ex-Etiquette for Weddings* to be our second ex-etiquette book because so many of the questions people ask us revolve around weddings. You'll see that this is much more than an etiquette book—it's an etiquette manual, wedding planner, parenting guide, and self-help book all rolled into one.

When Larry and I decided to marry, there was no protocol for getting married for the second time, so we just made it up as we went along. We got married at our home, not in a church, so many of the formal decisions associated with a church wedding were not issues for us. We included the kids in the wedding, which we decided to hold on New Year's Eve—a day symbolic of the transition from past to future.

We had a black-tie party. At 10:00 P.M. the minister arrived, we stopped the party, and the kids walked in wearing matching attire. Four years old at the time, my bonusson was excited that he was wearing a tux and staying up until ten. The minister married us using vows that we had written, and we all exchanged rings—adults and kids alike. I put the rings on my bonuschildren's fingers, and my husband put a ring on my daughter's finger.

The minister then announced to the guests, "Larry, Jann, Melanie, Anee, and Steven thank you for celebrating this wonderful occasion with them, and they welcome you all to their home." Then the first toast came—and my husband made it. My father had died months before and did not know that we were going to be married. My husband and my father had been longtime friends, and there was not a doubt in anyone's mind that Dad would have been happy about our union, so my husband spoke to him during the toast. It was a very sentimental, lovely toast. We lifted our glasses together, and then the party resumed—a built-in reception. In an hour or so, before the party got really crazy, my new parents-in-law took the kids home with them.

Planning my wedding was more stressful than it needed to be. I wish there had been a book at the time that addressed some of the decisions I faced. I had no idea what I was doing, nor was there anywhere to turn for help. I hope that *Ex-Etiquette for Weddings* becomes that book for others. Looking back, I would have done a lot of things differently—starting with communicating more with the other side of my bonuschildren's family. I should have talked to Sharyl about the changes we would all face after Larry and I married.

Now that our kids are older and have partners who might become spouses some day, there are a host of new considerations. Who will walk my daughter, Anee, down the aisle? My husband, Larry? Her father? Both of them? When my bonuschildren marry, what will be my place in their wedding planning? Where will I sit? Even though

Sharyl and I are now good friends, I'm still concerned that my active participation in the planning of my bonuschildren's weddings could offend her. Thank goodness we are good enough friends that if we faced that issue, we could talk about it. But for many people that's not the case, and the stress it causes can literally ruin their child's wedding day.

Life is not the same as when Emily Post wrote her first book of etiquette in 1922. Yesterday's rules for planning a wedding don't work when the ceremony attempts to join one of today's combined families. Nor will they work when the products of those combined families—the "yours, mine, and ours" kids—wish to get married. This means we need to establish a more contemporary approach to wedding planning, and that's how the rules of good ex-etiquette were born.

As you read through this book, you will notice that sometimes we use various words as catchalls. For example, we use the word *encore* to describe not only a second or subsequent marriage, but also the first marriage of someone who has a child from a previous relationship. Technically, we know that the latter is not an "encore" wedding, but when you have children, whether you married their other parent or not, you still face many of the same issues with your ex as do those who did marry.

We also use the word *divorce* as a catchall for couples who have split up. We know that some couples or parents never marry, and some are separated and not yet divorced. It's difficult to refer to every state of a relationship, so when talking about a breakup, most of the time we use the term *divorce*.

You may also notice that we usually use the word *bonus* in lieu of *step*. We began using the word in our early days as a combined family, as a more positive way to refer to the "step" experience. Personally, I didn't like being called a stepmother. It reminded me of an evil, wicked woman who resented the kids in her care, when I was doing everything in my power to be as kind and loving as I could possibly be to my stepchildren. To reinforce my discomfort with the word, one day my "stepdaughter," Melanie, confided that she did not like to introduce me as her stepmother because then her friends automatically thought she didn't like me. Thank goodness Sharyl's main concern was her daughter's comfort level. It enabled us to put our heads together and come up with another word to better describe the "step" relationship. The word we chose was *bonus*. A bonus is a reward for a job well done, and my husband's children were definitely a bonus in my life. Plus, *bonus* works quite well as a replacement—"bonusmom," rather than "stepmom," and "bonusdad," rather than "stepdad." "Blended mom" and "blended dad" just don't have the same ring, but, in order to not completely confuse our readers, we often use the words *bonus, blended,* and *step* interchangeably.

As a final note, you may notice that the voice in which this book is written is mine, Jann's. That's because it is very difficult for two people to write a book together, each in her own voice. We tried it, and the reader could not tell who was speaking. It became so confusing that we opted to use one combined voice. That voice ended up being mine because I'm the writer in the family. But you can be assured that Sharyl is no shrinking violet, and she has contributed to and reviewed every aspect of this book.

Sharyl and I make many personal appearances and teach Bonus Families and Ex-Etiquette workshops all over the country. If you would like to contact us to ask a question or to schedule a workshop, you can always do so through the Bonus Families Web site at www.bonusfamilies.com.

1

Laying the Groundwork

Divorce complicates just about everything, but above all—weddings. Whether it's your divorce, your parents', your sister's, or your friend's, divorce can turn the simplest wedding decision into a possible catastrophe. Why? Because the proper groundwork has not been laid for a divorced person to communicate with someone with whom he or she shares a stressful history. For many divorced people, the memories are so emotionally charged, and there is so much buried anger, that it's impossible to communicate with their exes without a flare-up.

At some point all of us have to interact with someone who conjures up unhappy, angry, or even bittersweet memories. Many times, divorce is at the root of those memories. This chapter prepares you for those interactions so you can approach them with an open mind and heart. "Laying the Groundwork" has little to do with preparing for the actual wedding. Instead, this chapter provides strategies to help you check your attitude so you can comfortably interact with an ex, an ex's family, bonuschildren, or divorced parents. These strategies are not just for the bride and groom. They're for anyone who must communicate with someone in the context of a breakup and remarriage, and who dreads the thought of it. As you read through these pages, you will see that "dreading the thought of it" may be the root of the problem.

I often hear:

> "*How can I plan my wedding? My parents are making what should be a wonderful time into a nightmare. My dad says he won't go if my mother and stepfather are there. My mother says she won't go if my dad is there.*"

or

> "*My fiancé has three children. His ex will not let them come to our wedding on the day I have chosen. He wants me to change the date! Who comes first? Me or his ex and the kids?*"

or

> "*I would like my niece—my divorced brother's daughter—to be my flower girl, but her mother says absolutely not! What do I do?*"

Each message is a plea for help from someone whose family has been touched by divorce. All three people feel that the situation is out of their control and that they are at the mercy of someone who doesn't respect them.

My advice to all of these people is to rely on what I call "good ex-etiquette"—good behavior after a divorce or separation.

What Is Ex-Etiquette?

"Etiquette" is simply a code of behavior based on politeness, kindness, and unselfishness. It's being gracious to those around us. Ex-etiquette applies those same rules of good behavior to an "ex" or past partner, or anyone affiliated with a past partner. And that means anyone's past partner—yours, your parent's, your child's, your sister's, your friend's—anyone who is trying to navigate rocky social waters after a breakup.

Using good ex-etiquette will enable you to interact productively with people with whom you share a painful or worrisome past. It will allow you to remain cordial and make the logical decisions that need to be made when planning a wedding. Ex-etiquette will *not* solve the issues or emotions that originally caused the animosity. In other words, using good ex-etiquette may help you politely discuss the jealousy you feel, but it won't cure the jealousy. That is something the person who feels the jealousy must work through on his or her own.

This is when many people cringe. Few feel obliged to be kind or polite to a past partner or the relative of a past partner, especially if the breakup was nasty. That's when I hear:

> *"Be serious. I got a divorce years ago. I never have to talk to my ex or my ex's relatives."*

This comment is typical of a divorced person. In my work as a mediator, I hear it every day: "I'm divorced. It's over. Don't bother me." For some people, particularly those without kids, this may be true. One of the partners picks up and leaves, and you never hear from that person again. However, if you have kids it's probably a different story. Joint custody has become the most common form of child custody awarded to parents after divorce or separation. Some divorced parents take it one step further and share physical custody, which means the kids go back and forth between the parents' homes on a regular basis. If divorced parents co-parent their children, they can no longer walk away from each other after a breakup. Much to many a divorced parent's dismay, that means *it's never over*. Not if you want to do it right. You will always share children, grandchildren, and if you are very lucky, great-grandchildren.

Nevertheless, I typically hear:

"But my child is an adult—over eighteen. I no longer have to deal with my ex."

or

"I'm over eighteen, finally an adult. Thank goodness all this will finally end."

It's a common misconception. Some people feel that once a child turns eighteen, she is no longer the responsibility of her parent or stepparent. If there was trouble coping with divorce or blending families as the child was growing, at eighteen you can consider the trouble over. Few consider the future after the child of divorce becomes an adult—not even the child herself. But very likely, when this adult child chooses to marry, there will be a wedding that both parents and extended families must attend.

Planning a wedding should be one of the most exciting times in a person's life, but for children of divorce it's often filled with anxiety—not necessarily about tying the knot, although some children of divorce do harbor a fear of getting married themselves—but about once again being put right in the middle of their parents' bickering and attempts to either alienate or control. The child of divorce is always jockeying for position—aligning with Dad when with Dad, aligning with Mom when with Mom. Although this is painful, most people in this position understand how to navigate those waters. But there is one factor that typically makes that balancing act possible: the fact that the parents are not in each other's presence for any length of time. Planning a wedding in which both parents will take an active role—parents who haven't gotten along for years and may have even remarried, but who will now be forced to appear together in public *and cooperate*—sends chills down the back of many a first-time bride or groom. As a child of divorce said:

> *"Will you please tell my parents that they are supposed to be polite to each other when I am around? They have put me in the middle of their battles for years. It's exhausting to be around either of them."*

If you are divorced, or if your parents are divorced, and you want to continue to share the major milestones of your lives, you must realize that when a child turns eighteen it's just another chapter, not the end of the book. Understanding this changes everything. As a result, a whole new type of communication must be developed. That's where ex-etiquette comes in.

The Ten Rules of Good Ex-Etiquette for Weddings

We are often asked if there are any formal rules for good ex-etiquette —something to refer to, like the Ten Commandments when you have questions about the proper attitude toward or response to a situation. As a result, in our first book, *Ex-Etiquette for Parents: Good*

Behavior After a Divorce or Separation, we offer ten rules of good ex-etiquette to help guide parents toward better co-parenting after divorce. In this book we offer a similar list for those who are facing a wedding when there has been a divorce in the family:

1. Remember whose wedding it is.
2. Ask for help if you need it.
3. Never badmouth the bride, groom, extended family members, or guests.
4. Offer advice only if you are asked. Even then, remember "tact and timing."
5. Don't be spiteful.
6. Don't hold grudges.
7. Use empathy when problem solving. Put yourself in the other person's place.
8. Be honest and straightforward.
9. Respect each other's family traditions, histories, and allegiances.
10. Compromise whenever possible. Look for solutions outside of the box.

How to Communicate Effectively with Your Ex

Why would you need to communicate effectively with your ex when there is a wedding in the works? There are a couple of scenarios. As I discussed earlier, maybe you have children together. If you are remarrying, or your ex is remarrying, that remarriage will certainly affect the children. Whatever affects your children is the business of both you and your ex, and you will need to communicate productively with one another about the issues that affect them. Or maybe your adult child is getting married. Then you and your ex will need to get along to make your child's wedding day the best it can possibly be.

There are five actions or behaviors that will help you and your ex interact successfully:

1. Stop assigning blame and decide to cooperate.
2. Break the old patterns of communication.
3. Let go of negative emotions.
4. Realize that holding on to the past prevents positive present interaction.
5. Acknowledge your mutual interests.

Stop Assigning Blame and Decide to Cooperate

I often hear people object, "But I do cooperate! It's not me. It's him!" It's rarely *only* the other person. It may be true that you are not contributing to the immediate communication problem, but there was probably a time in the past when you did. Believe it or not, your ex hasn't forgotten. During an interaction you might be thinking, "I was just very polite, and his response was really rude!" Meanwhile he's thinking, "Yeah, she was nice just now, but five years ago when I asked for _____ [you fill in the blank], she was really miserable to me. I'm justified in being rude now. It's her fault."

Assigning blame is really just an excuse for bad behavior. You get stuck feeling justified in your anger and feeling like a wounded individual—and then you seek revenge, which *really* prevents positive communication. Revenge doesn't have to be the type of revenge you see in the movies, where people plot with guns or poison. It can be in the form of being uncooperative with your ex. That hurts the other person more than physical revenge—and lasts far longer. You win. Or do you?

It's time to stop using *rights*, *sides*, *fault*, and *blame* as reasons for bad behavior and to take responsibility for your own actions. That's why I say that deciding to cooperate, despite whose "fault" you think something is, is the first step to positive interaction.

Break the Old Patterns of Communication

Breaking an old pattern of communication is not easy. So much of it is mental preparation. When you prepare for a meeting with your ex by stewing about how he has made you angry, or worrying that something you might say will make him angry, the thoughts that you run over and over in your mind will have an effect when you finally interact. Negative thought can lead to negative behavior. In the psychological community this is referred to as a "conditioned response based on past experiences." If your thoughts about someone conjure up feelings of anger and resentment or worry and anxiety, you are not likely to want to cooperate. If you can change your thinking process, you can change your behavior.

I often tell a personal story that's a perfect example of how thought processes affect a person's behavior—and what that person must do to break the cycle. It's about communicating with my husband's ex, not my own, but the relationship was perhaps just as emotionally charged. My husband and I had been married for six months, and during that time Sharyl and I were not the best of friends. Every morning I would sit in front of my makeup mirror, and as I put on my makeup, I'd rehearse what I was going to say to her the next time she did something that made me angry. As I put on my foundation, I was a little miffed. As I progressed to the blusher, I was angrier still. By the time I was adding the finishing touches with my mascara, I was livid—and I hadn't said a thing to anyone!

This went on day after day. I thought I was keeping it all inside and that no one knew how angry I was, until one day my husband timidly tiptoed around the corner of the bathroom.

"What are you doing?" I snapped.

"Well," he relied, "I was checking to see how much makeup you're wearing. It seems the more makeup you have on, the angrier you are with me."

I had no idea my husband was so perceptive, and I was very impressed. His comment made me realize that *I* was the one making me angry, not Sharyl. As soon as I sat down in front of my mirror each morning, I started with the same vengeful, angry thought process. It was simply learned behavior—I had taught myself to be angry!

Since I had learned to be angry, I decided I could learn *not* to be angry, too. Rather than rehearse all the bad things in my head each morning, I made myself think about the good things—how happy I was to be married to my husband, that everyone was healthy, and that the kids had accepted me and seemed to be adjusting so well. Every time a bad thought came into my mind about Sharyl, I pushed it out and replaced it with a more positive thought about my life.

Lo and behold, the next time my husband crept around the bathroom corner, I said, "Hi, Honey!" rather than growling at him. But, equally important, the next time I spoke to Sharyl, I didn't have one bad thing to say to her. And oddly enough, she didn't have one bad thing to say to me either. We had changed our pattern of communication.

I had been thoroughly convinced that it was Sharyl's fault that we were at odds. If I had not made the necessary changes in myself to break the negative thought chain and to change those negative expectations into positive affirmations, I would still be furious— sitting in front of my mirror and snapping at everyone who crossed my path.

This is when people tell me, "I can't do this all by myself. Doesn't it take two to communicate?" Like most people, you have probably been taught that communication is a two-way street. If one party does not wish to communicate, then it is unlikely things will change, right? Wrong. Communication doesn't start with two people. It starts with one person: you. Things *can* change when only one person is committed to change. Rather than try to change your ex's mind, or your parent's mind, or the mind of anyone with whom you have not gotten along in the past, what you really have to do is change your own mind—change your own belief about your "opponent." As a result, you will now have control over your own life.

Remember, positive affirmations are always true statements, but they may not be the first thoughts that come to your mind. They are thoughts *you* hold onto in order to stop *your* negative behaviors.

Negative thought: *My ex is so difficult!*
Positive affirmation: *My ex and I both love our child.*

Positive affirmations do not necessarily have to be about the problem at hand. Any positive thought works to break the negative thought/negative behavior chain of events. It's the dwelling on the negative that makes you react negatively. Dwell on the positive and you will react positively.

Let Go of Negative Emotions

The emotions that are most troublesome when dealing with an ex are resentment, jealousy, and envy. On some level, all are natural responses to fear. Reason goes right out the window, and what becomes most important is defending one's position. Conquering these emotions is a prerequisite of good ex-etiquette. Controlling negative emotions doesn't mean you don't feel them. Good ex-etiquette provides tools to deal with interacting with an ex when you *do* feel angry, jealous, or resentful.

This may sound like denial. You are in denial when you don't see or accept something. It's a *subconscious* coping mechanism for avoiding something painful. I am suggesting that you deal with something by *consciously* changing your thinking. That's not denial. That's "the wisdom to know the difference."

To combat jealousy, for example, start thinking of your ex solely as your children's father or mother. He or she is a parent, not a past lover. When you speak or think about your ex, refer to him or her as "Bill's [your child's] mother or father," not "my ex-wife or ex-husband."

This works with other relationships too. Refer to "Susan's [your husband's daughter from a previous marriage] mother," rather than "my husband's ex-wife." Or, if you are a child of divorce, rather than looking at your stepparent as a possible replacement for your parent, try thinking of him or her as someone who simply makes your other parent happy—and let it go.

Realize That Holding on to the Past Prevents Present Interaction

> *"I've tried to reason with my ex. It's a complete waste of time. Now our child is getting married, and I know he won't cooperate."*

This person thinks she's speaking from experience, but really, she's just holding on to the past. Let's say you have a friend who has a cat. The cat was recently lost, and when it returned home it was a little disoriented. You think you know the cat pretty well, but when you come over to see your friend, the cat scratches you. Let's analyze what your response might be. You might yell at the cat, and it would perceive you as being angry. You might lash out or smack it on the nose. At that point the cat would know that you are angry, and it might growl and get into a fighting stance to warn you not to do that again. The next time you see the cat, you are on the defensive—you don't want to be scratched again. When the cat sees you, it remembers that you smacked it in the nose; now it starts growling out of fear as soon as it sees you. You are afraid that you will once again be scratched, and you get into your fighting stance.

Your relationships with people are no different. People are afraid to be vulnerable or hurt. It's not uncommon for an ex to mistake your fear for anger and to respond accordingly. Good communication doesn't just happen. *You* have to set the stage, which means mentally washing the slate clean of past experiences and walking into each meeting with an open mind. Just keep doing it until you have conditioned yourself to both expect and participate in good post-divorce behavior. Then you will have finally let go of the past.

Acknowledge Your Mutual Interests

Most people who face conflict with each other spend their time examining their differences, not the things they have in common. And yet, mutual interests are the building blocks for agreement and good behavior. Ask yourself, "What do we both want?" There *will* be something, from "giving the child we both love a beautiful wedding" to "making my children or my fiancé's children feel safe in our union." The common interest of all the players can be found if all search their hearts and make someone other than themselves of primary importance.

Putting Ex-Etiquette into Practice: When an Adult Child of Divorce Marries

Here is a story to which children of divorce planning a wedding can relate. We will apply the rules of good ex-etiquette and see how the outcome can be positive, rather than negative, and how the stage can be set for positive future interactions.

"*My mom and dad have been divorced for years and do not talk much. I announced my engagement last month and just found the wedding dress of my dreams. When I told my mom how much it was, she went white. She told me she couldn't afford it and suggested I ask my dad. This is so awkward! Why am I always in the middle?"*

No child, no matter her age, wants to be put in the middle of Mom and Dad, but divorced parents often use their children as their intermediaries. Anticipating that interaction with an ex will be a problem, they take the easy way out and ask their child to pass on important information. It starts when the children are young—"Tell your mom I won't pick you up until 7:00 next time"; "Tell your dad your practice has been cancelled"—and will continue into adulthood if not nipped in the bud. To make matters worse, if the information passed on by the child makes the parent angry, the child feels as if he or she has done something wrong. It's a huge burden for children, one that gets no easier as the child grows older.

Younger children of divorce can be taught to politely suggest that their parents work it out between themselves. This will take them out of the middle and actually empower their parents to be more responsible. "Mom, I may forget. It is important that you tell Dad that my practice is cancelled." Adult children planning a wedding can say something like, "Please coordinate efforts with Dad so I know how much I can spend on flowers." Just by saying those few simple words, a bride has put quite a few of the rules for good ex-etiquette into practice. First, she has used rule number eight, "Be honest and straightforward." Her behavior also prevents badmouthing between divorced parents, and "Never badmouth" is rule number three. Being equally upfront with Mom and Dad stops any possible tit-for-tat behavior on their part, which is what rule number five, "Don't be spiteful," addresses. Furthermore, the bride's straightforward behavior supports her positive allegiance to both her mother and father, and that's exactly what I am talking about in rule number nine, "Respect each other's family traditions, histories, and *allegiances*." Finally, by politely asking Dad and Mom to coordinate efforts, this bride has set the stage for compromise—rule number ten, "Compromise whenever possible"—and lets her parents know that she both desires and expects their cooperation.   It's amazing, by using one simple sentence, this bride has employed five of the ten rules of good ex-etiquette.

Putting Ex-Etiquette into Practice: From the Parents' Point of View

Now let's examine the same story above, but this time from the mother-of-the-bride's point of view. She feels she has no ulterior motive other than lack of funds. But if the father can't afford the dress either, it is now *his* responsibility to give their daughter the final "no." He ends up being the bad guy, not Mom. It's obvious that the daughter has been put between her mom and dad in the past and doesn't like it one bit.

Using good ex-etiquette, how should the mother of the bride deal with this situation? Although the mother refers to a budget, it does not appear that there has ever been a formal plan in place to address the extras her child might need as she grows. Now faced with paying for a wedding, the mother employs the same tactic she always did: "I can't afford it. See if your dad can."

Using the rules of good ex-etiquette, don't tell the child to ask her other parent. Say something like, "I'll figure something out," and put her on hold. Call the other parent, explain the situation, and together look for a solution to the problem. By doing this you are employing *all* of the rules of good ex-etiquette for weddings:

1. Remember whose wedding it is.
   The mother is approaching the problem with the child's best interest in mind.

2. Ask for help if you need it.

   The mother is reaching out to the ex for assistance.

3. Never badmouth extended family.

   Taking this approach eliminates talking behind someone's back or degrading them in front of other family members.

4. Offer advice only if you are asked.

   Mom is not really offering advice, but she is making a suggestion on how to handle the situation.

5. Don't be spiteful.

6. Don't hold grudges.

   Mom has let go of the past in order to find a solution. She is approaching her daughter's father with an open mind and will not be spiteful nor hold a grudge in her interaction with him.

7. Use empathy when problem solving.

   The mother is putting herself in her ex's place. No one wants to be embarrassed or put on the spot—especially in front of the children.

8. Be honest and straightforward.

   This approach eliminates all the back-biting and tit-for-tat behavior and sets the stage for future positive interaction.

9. Respect family traditions, histories, and allegiances.

   The mother is offering respect, in her manner and attitude, toward both her daughter and her ex. This will help her ex to stay open to her suggestions.

10. Compromise whenever possible.

    Mom recognizes that neither she nor her ex can afford the dress on their own, so they must compromise.

Here are some more divorced-parents-of-the-bride scenarios:

"*One time I asked my ex for help with some medical coverage for our daughter, and he said no. I didn't realize he had his own financial problems at the time. Years went by. I resented that first 'no' and did not want to put myself in that vulnerable place again. But when our daughter announced she was getting married, I decided to try again. I told my ex how difficult it was for me to ask for his financial help because I had done it once before and he had said no. His response? 'I did? When?' He had been so overwhelmed with his own money troubles at the time, he didn't remember my asking.*

'You should have asked again,' he said. 'I would have helped.'

'You should have volunteered,' I said. 'I asked once.'

'But I didn't remember later,' he said. 'I was just concerned that I continued to pay child support on time.'

'Didn't remember? That your daughter needed medical coverage?'

'When you never brought it up again, I thought it was handled and forgot about it.'"

You can see how both parents had their own issues on this subject, and it was perpetuated by their preconceived notions, which confused their decision-making process. When they started talking about it, they realized they both could have communicated more effectively in the past, and they decided to split the cost of the wedding. Sound ridiculously simple? It does if you get along. But if you don't, and if you cringe at the thought of even *talking* to your ex-spouse, then this solution is not the first thing to come to your mind. That's when it is particularly helpful to rely on the rules of good ex-etiquette. When you are stressed, agitated, or overwhelmed, having these reminders to let the grudge go, to avoid spitefulness, or to put yourself in the other's place, will help you to rise above the chaos and find solutions.

"My ex and I have three kids, and the oldest child has just announced her engagement. I never stayed in contact with my ex's side of the family. Do I have to talk to these people at the wedding?"

Yes, you do. Even though *you* didn't stay in contact with your ex's family after the divorce, your child probably did. Let's put this question into the proper perspective. Essentially, you are asking if you have to talk to your child's aunt, uncle, cousins, and grandparents at your child's wedding. When you look at it that way, the answer is obvious. If you are all invited to the wedding, and you all choose to attend, then you act cordially. That is, if you want your child to have a lovely day to remember. If you want to color your child's day with spite, anger, and revenge, and offer no role model for resolving conflict or for positive adult relationships, then boycott the ceremony and refuse to speak to your ex-relatives. But that's certainly not good ex-etiquette, and it's downright bad parenting.

It's important to note that good ex-etiquette does not demand that you have long conversations reminiscing about the past with someone whom you may regard as your enemy. It does demand, however, cordial public behavior for the sake of the child getting married. If you simply act cordially at your child's wedding, you are following all the rules of good ex-etiquette, but most specifically, rule number nine, "Respect each other's family traditions, histories, and allegiances." A child of divorce spends time with Mom and time with Dad. He or she has two families and has formed separate family histories and allegiances over the years. It's not uncommon for divorced parents to forget this and think that their side of the family is their child's primary concern. This forces the child to check his or her allegiances, and things can get very uncomfortable at family get-togethers, like weddings, when both sides of the family are present. With this in mind, divorced parents must be sensitive to the allegiances and the history their child has formed with their other parent. This is done by doing things like remaining cordial at events that are important to their child—especially their wedding.

Laying the Groundwork for Remarriage with Children

"My fiancé and I are engaged and plan to marry in a few months. We both have children from previous marriages, and we have moved in together. He shares custody of his children with his ex. We are having a little trouble with the blending process, but I am sure everything will fall into place once we get married, right?"

This is a common trap—thinking that once you are officially married, everything will fall into place. However, if there are problems before you marry, signing a piece of paper and going through a ceremony will not eliminate them. More than planning your wedding, you need to lay the groundwork for your marriage.

One way to lay the groundwork for a blended family is to make a family plan. Find a pen, some paper, and a quiet place with your partner. Before addressing the practical things—who washes the dishes on Tuesdays, who cleans up after the dog—you need to create a positive mental picture of your new family. Begin by envisioning the relationship you want to foster with each new family member. Write each name on the piece of paper. Under each name, list what you will do to make that relationship as positive and fruitful as possible. Start with your new partner and then go through each member of your new family. For example:

Larry [my partner's name]

I will discuss my feelings before my anger clouds my reason.

I will not place him in a position where he must choose between his children and me.

I will stick to the disciplinary rules we make.

I will not undermine his authority in front of the children (no matter whose children they are).

Doing this exercise with your partner for every member of the family helps both of you to organize your thoughts and get a clear idea of what you expect in your life together. Discuss everything—even subjects you think are taboo, like favoritism, discipline, or dealing with the ex—because those are the subjects that will inevitably tear you apart when you have no plan in place for how you will deal with them. After the adults have a clear idea of what is expected, it's a good idea to get the kids into the act. A family discussion that asks them how they will foster positive relationships will help them to see how their new family can be a positive force in their lives.

Now that we have laid the groundwork for positive communication when divorce is part of the picture, and have seen a few examples of putting good ex-etiquette into practice, let's move on. It's time to announce that engagement!

2

Your Engagement

nnouncing your engagement should be an exciting time, but it can be fraught with stressful anticipation when family members are battling. Couples with divorced parents wonder which parent they should tell first. Couples with children from previous marriages wonder what the proper protocol is for telling their kids. And then there's the question of the proper wording on those engagement announcements! This chapter will help you deal with all these issues and then some.

Announcing Your Engagement When Your Parents Are Divorced

If you have never been married, and neither you nor your intended have children from a previous relationship, protocol suggests that the first people you tell are your parents. Begin by notifying the bride's parents. If they are divorced, tell the custodial parent first (the parent with whom the bride spent the most time growing up), and then move on to the non-custodial parent. If both parents shared custody equally, the decision about whom to call first is up to you. To help you make that decision, you can always fall back on traditional wedding protocol that dictates that the mother is generally given the "top" spot. As you read through this book, you will see several examples of this: If divorced parents cannot get along, a divorced mom is seated in the first row at the wedding ceremony, and Dad sits in the second. A divorced mom is listed on the first line on wedding invitations, whereas Dad is listed on the second, etc.

The next people to receive a call are the groom's parents. If they are divorced, again start with the custodial parent.

Next in line would be the bride's grandparents, then the groom's grandparents, then the bride's extended family, then the groom's extended family. Then move through your list of friends.

Announcing Your Encore Wedding

Telling Your Ex

If you and your ex do not have children, there's no need to tell him or her that you are remarrying, unless you still stay in contact because you share assets—a business, for example. The etiquette is different, however, if children are involved.

If you are remarrying and have adult children, tell your children first. Then tell your ex during the natural course of telling family and friends. This prevents any potential embarrassment if exes continue to share friends after the divorce or if both must attend a family get-together accompanied by new spouses. If you are remarrying and share custody of your *young* children with your ex, then it will be a well-choreographed dance of telling the ex and the children at approximately the same time. I know this may be different from anything you have ever heard or read about in an etiquette book, but the support of your ex, even in the smallest fashion, will go a long way toward helping your child adjust to the idea of Mommy or Daddy marrying again. Here's a question and response that illustrates the importance of this strategy:

> *"My ex-wife and I have a six-year-old son. Although he lives primarily with his mother, I see him every weekend. This weekend he walked in the door and announced, 'Mommy is getting married! I'm the ring bearer!' I didn't even know she was dating anyone! I don't want to make waves with my ex, because we get along pretty well, but I'm furious that my son gave me the news instead of his mother. This can't be good ex-etiquette, can it?"*

No, it's not good ex-etiquette. If this ex-wife is like hundreds of others with whom I have spoken, she probably thought her upcoming marriage was none of her ex-husband's business. But in this case, that's not true. If a divorced couple is attempting to co-parent, then both homes in which the child lives are equally important, and when something important happens at either home, it is vital that the parents share that information, for the sake of their child.

Power struggles are quite common among divorced parents. And what serves as the bartering chip in this struggle for power? Information. Whoever knows more, wins. Don't tell your ex that Billy has Little League practice on Saturday. Don't volunteer that he loves to cook at your house. "You didn't know that Billy loved to cook? Well, what kind of parent are you?" Whoever has the most information is the most in control—and therefore has the most power.

If you follow this line of reasoning, withholding information about upcoming marriage plans is to be expected. But good ex-etiquette suggests that when you have decided to remarry, your ex should be informed around the same time as the children, so he or she can support your decision to marry, rather than undermine it. That way, when your child comes home with an announcement like, "Mommy's getting married!" your ex's response can be, "Yes, I know, Honey. And I hear you are going to be a ring bearer in the ceremony. You must be very excited. . . ." rather than, "What? That #@%^&! I had no idea!" Which response do you think will make the child feel more comfortable and secure?

Telling your ex about your remarriage needn't be a traumatic event. If you have been following the rules of good ex-etiquette, the fact that you are remarrying will not be a surprise to your ex. He or she will have already met your new partner, and, as tough as it may be, past and present partners will be doing their best to put their issues aside for the sake of the children in their care.

In a perfect world, a parent who plans to remarry would tell his or her ex the news a short time before telling their children. If possible, schedule a time when all the adults—you, your intended, and your ex—can meet without the children present. If you anticipate the meeting will be awkward, nothing more than cordial introductions and basic information need be exchanged.

Even if you live far away, a letter or phone call is in order. It can be a short, concise letter or call. Just talk about the subject at hand. No embellishments are necessary. Here's an example of an appropriate letter:

Dear Michael,

I wanted to tell you first that Robert and I have decided to marry soon. I will be telling the children within the week. I want to assure you that my goal is to make the transition as easy as possible on the kids and to continue to co-parent alongside you in the best interests of our children.

Sincerely,

Michelle

If you are talking on the phone, the language need not be so formal. The goal is to notify your ex of your impending marriage and let him or her know that you want to continue to put the children first, now and always.

> *"I've been married for a year to a man who has a seven-year-old son from a previous marriage. Though I've never met my husband's ex-wife, we see my stepson every weekend, and I take care of him most of the time when he's at our home. On Sunday we dropped him off at his mother's house. My husband walked up to the door with his son, and they went into the house while I waited in the car. My husband soon came out but continued to talk to his ex at the door. I felt very uncomfortable. Would it have been too aggressive if I got out of the car to meet her? Would it have been more appropriate if my husband introduced me?"*

What would have been the best ex-etiquette would have been for your husband to announce his engagement and introduce you to his child's mother back when the two of you decided on a future together. That way, you could have openly expressed your desire to support both parents in their efforts to make this child's life as stress-free as possible—and set the stage for working together in the future. As it is, no groundwork was laid for future communication, and I'm not surprised you felt uncomfortable. If any two people understand how difficult it is to converse with your partner's ex or your ex's new partner, Sharyl and I do. For years we dreaded talking to each other—but we learned out of necessity.

First step? You meet each other. Yes, all three in the same room! If and when his ex-wife gets engaged, expect another such meeting with the roles reversed. Remember to be cordial. They will feel as awkward as you do right now.

Telling Your Younger Children

If you have laid the proper groundwork as an encore couple, it should not come as a surprise to your kids that you are discussing marriage. The response will be different if, on the other hand, you meet and become engaged in a short period of time. In cases like these, the kids may still be mourning the initial divorce and may not be open to another person in their lives. Add to that the fact that they may feel concern about the welfare of their other biological parent, and possibly about having to move or share a room with a new sibling they barely know, and I can guarantee the reception will be less than favorable.

Most people understand that adults need a courting period before they decide to marry, but few apply that same reasoning to relationships with the children. Telling the kids about your decision to marry will be their first indication of what is to come when you unite as husband and wife. After you are married, will you include them, or will it be you two against them? The way that you handle being in this new relationship and present the news of your upcoming nuptials will give them an idea.

When you announce your engagement to your young children, make sure you explain everything thoroughly and use age-appropriate language that they will understand. Don't be surprised if you have to repeat yourself, or explain the same concept in another way, to calm their fears. It is imperative that you use tact, and time your announcement appropriately (ex-etiquette for weddings rule number four).

Parents sometimes take it for granted that kids understand the meaning behind common words associated with marriage—and they may not. I often tell the story of one family I worked with in which the four-year-old daughter had seen a wedding only on TV. It was a hot-air-balloon theme wedding; the couple was married as the balloon sailed over Napa Valley. The girl had been frightened by the fire used to raise the balloon, and from then on she thought that a wedding meant you had to go up in a balloon with fire. As you can imagine, her reaction to her mother's announcement that she was getting married was less than favorable.

I worked with another child who did not understand what a "honeymoon" was. He was told Mommy was going on her "honeymoon" after she and "Bill" were married, and he was to stay with Bill's parents. But he wasn't told how long the honeymoon would last, and he thought he was now going to have to *live* with his new bonusgrandparents. Based on that, even though he liked Bill very much, he did not want Mommy to get married. It took quite a while to figure out what was going on in his mind.

Remarriage is an important step—one that often sets children back if it's not handled properly. Here's a new concept: if your child is excited about you or your ex remarrying, it's a sign that you have all done something right. His excitement is telling you he feels comfortable in both homes. And what better legacy can you pass on to your child than for him to understand he is a loved and active member of a loving family—in this case, two loving families? You have done your job well.

Telling Your Adult Children

Many older couples anticipate that their adult children will just be "reasonable" about their wedding plans because, as adults, they should understand the desire to have a life partner. As a result, many people don't take the same care to integrate new partners when their children are adults as they would if their children were young.

> *"I was married for twenty-five years and have two adult kids.*
> *I've recently begun seeing a wonderful man who lost his wife*
> *of thirty-two years from cancer six years ago. We get along*
> *great and plan to marry soon. The problem is, his children,*
> *who are all in their thirties with kids of their own, are not*
> *accepting their dad's decision to move on. They have been*

nasty to him, saying things like 'How can you do this to Mom?' This makes him feel very guilty, and I fear it may be the beginning of the end for us. I am to the point where I don't want to be around his kids anymore, and he thinks they won't even come to our wedding. Help!"

Adult children have just as many concerns as younger kids when it comes to a parent's remarriage. First, they have had more time with their deceased or divorced parent and have formed long-term allegiances and memories. If divorced or widowed parents go too fast into the wonderful world of dating, their adult children may see it as a betrayal of their other parent. And, like younger children, adult children may also feel guilty if they find that they like their parent's choice, which may prevent them bonding with their parent's new partner.

Second, adult children are also more conscious of issues surrounding the inheritance of property. Without proper estate planning, if a parent dies, family heirlooms and property are transferred to the current spouse. That spouse then has the responsibility of distributing the deceased parent's property. If the deceased parent hasn't made his or her wishes known through a will or trust, the surviving partner may think he or she knows the wishes of the deceased, but may be mistaken. Adult children are often concerned that family heirlooms or property may not get to the proper child or relative.

There are other considerations as well. Older surviving spouses may feel as if they don't have the luxury of a long courtship—it may seem like a waste of precious time together with their new spouse. And, like their kids, they think they know their own mind and want to move at their own pace. Adult children, still in mourning, may simply resent their parent's ability to move on and may resent the new partner for no other reason than that he or she is not Mom or Dad.

The woman who wrote this letter hasn't mentioned how long she has been dating her gentleman friend, but it sounds as if they moved rather quickly. Even if it has been six years since "Mom" died, a new relationship and quick engagement is still probably a shock to the kids. The question, "How can you do this to Mom?" could be an indicator that the kids have yet to truly accept that Mom is gone and also can't accept that Dad is ready to move on.

This father has to make it clear to his kids that someone new is not a replacement for Mom. The new person is his chosen companion at this time of his life. Of course he would not have written the story the way it turned out, but he's grateful to have found someone now that he likes so much. Dad may also want to suggest that his kids not devalue the memory of their mother by comparing his relationship with a new partner to his relationship with their mother. The women are two different people, and these are two different relationships. Comparing does a disservice to their mother's memory and to his new love, and may make it impossible for him to build a relationship with someone who makes him happy.

Telling the Rest of the Family

"After the ex and the kids, then whom should we tell?"

Next on the list are the bride's parents, then the groom's parents, then the extended family. As you talk about the upcoming nuptials, don't forget to ask them for their support. If you have kids, and your other relatives are not happy about your remarriage, let them know that their unhappiness should be voiced to you, not your children, and that attempting to undermine a union that is inevitable by voicing their discontent to the children will only strain their future relationships with you, your new partner, and your kids.

Announcing Your Engagement in the Newspaper

Announcing an engagement in the newspaper is usually done for first marriages, but it is not improper to announce a second marriage, especially if only one partner has been married before. It should not be announced before your engagement party, however, and it most commonly appears in the paper about two or three months before the scheduled date of the marriage. If you are really planning ahead, it is perfectly all right to announce an engagement up to a year ahead of time. Announcement information should be sent to your newspaper's "lifestyles" editor at least two weeks before you wish it to appear. Note that not all papers publish engagement announcements for free; there may be a small fee.

Some papers have a specific form they like you to use when submitting an engagement or wedding announcement, so before you go to the trouble of preparing your own announcement, check with them first. Make it a point not to include information that is too personal— your address, for example, for fear of someone breaking into your home to search for wedding bounty. Below you will find some suggestions for wording of announcements depending on your life situation. Let's say Mary Smith and James Miller would like to announce their engagement.

Announcements If Your Parents Are Divorced

If your parents are divorced, the parent you lived with makes the announcement, but both parents are mentioned. When in doubt, list the bride's mother first. In this example, the bride-to-be, Mary Smith, lives with her mother:

> *Mrs. Louise Smith of Brentwood, California, announces the engagement of her daughter, Mary Smith, to James Miller, the son of Mr. & Mrs. Robert Miller of Houston, Texas. Miss Smith is also the daughter of Dr. John Smith of Detroit, Michigan.*

Then add education and work references and the month for which the wedding is planned.

If your parents are divorced but still friendly, they may choose to announce together:

Dr. John Smith of Detroit, Michigan, and Mrs. Louise Smith of Brentwood, California, announce the engagement of their daughter, Mary Smith, to James Miller, the son of Mr. & Mrs. Robert Miller of Houston, Texas.

If your mother has remarried, and she uses her current married name, Mrs. Louise Cornwall:

Mr. & Mrs. George Cornwall of Brentwood, California, announce the engagement of Mrs. Cornwall's daughter, Mary Smith, to James Miller, the son of Mr. & Mrs. Robert Miller of Houston, Texas. Miss Mary Smith is also the daughter of Dr. John Smith of Detroit, Michigan.

In this case, the listing of the father's name is just protocol; he is not announcing the engagement. This type of announcement would be for divorced parents who might not interact with each other on a regular basis. Perhaps the biological father did not take an active part in the child's upbringing, and the bonusdad has taken on the "dad" role, but the daughter, or possibly the remarried mother, or even the bonusdad, still wants to acknowledge the biological father in the announcement.

If both parents have remarried and everyone is cordial:

Mr. & Mrs. Michael Baldwin of Brentwood, California, and Dr. & Mrs. John Smith of Detroit, Michigan, announce the engagement of Mrs. Baldwin's and Dr. Smith's daughter, Mary

*Smith, to Mr. James Miller, son of Mr. & Mrs. Robert Miller
of Houston, Texas.*

If only one parent has remarried and announces with his or her
current spouse and the other biological parent:

*Mr. & Mrs. George Cornwall of Brentwood, California, and
Dr. John Smith, of Detroit, Michigan, announce the engagement of Mrs. Cornwall and Dr. Smith's daughter, Mary Smith,
to James Miller, the son of Mr. & Mrs. Robert Miller of Houston, Texas.*

Announcing Your Own Engagement When Your Parents Are Divorced

*Mary Ann Smith, of Brentwood, California, and James Michael
Miller of Houston, Texas, announce their engagement. The
couple plans a November wedding in Brentwood, California.*

*The bride-to-be is the daughter of Mrs. Louise Cornwall of
Brentwood, California, and Dr. John Smith of Detroit, Michi-
gan. The future bridegroom is the son of Mr. & Mrs. Robert
Miller of Houston, Texas.*

Announcements If One or Both Parents Are Deceased

Here, the father of the bride has passed away:

*The engagement of Miss Mary Smith, daughter of Mrs. Louise
Smith and the late Dr. John Smith of Brentwood, California,
to James Miller, son of Mr. & Mrs. Robert Miller of Houston,
Texas, is announced by the bride's mother.*

If both of your parents are deceased, then an aunt or uncle or other close relative can make the announcement:

> *Mr. Michael Hensley of Boston, Massachusetts, announces the engagement of his niece, Miss Mary Smith, to Mr. James Miller, son of Mr. & Mrs. Robert Miller of Houston, Texas. Miss Smith is the daughter of the late Dr. & Mrs. John Smith, of Brentwood, California.*

Announcing Your Own Encore Engagement

"Is it appropriate to formally announce an encore engagement?"

That really depends on how many engagements (and marriages) there have been. There is no issue when announcing a second engagement. However, if there have been multiple marriages, the more discreet the better. If it's the groom's second or subsequent marriage but the *bride's* first marriage, then the engagement announcement may be treated as a first wedding. The wording would be similar to children of divorced parents announcing their own engagement; only in this case, the bride's name may be different because she's been married before:

> *Mary Ann Maloney, of Brentwood, California, and James Michael Miller of Houston, Texas, announce their engagement. The couple plans a November wedding in Brentwood, California.*

Parents Announcing Your Encore Wedding Engagement

While most encore couples announce their marriages today, parents may do so, if they wish.

Dr. & Mrs. John Smith of Brentwood, California, announce the engagement of their daughter, Mary Mahoney, to Mr. James Miller, son of Mr. & Mrs. Robert Miller of Houston, Texas.

Mary Mahoney may want to include her maiden name, Mary *Smith* Mahoney. Previously it was optional to also include, "Mary Mahoney's [or Ms. Mahoney's] first marriage ended in divorce." But today there is no need to mention the way anyone's previous marriage ended, in an engagement announcement.

Engagement Parties

"My boyfriend and I have decided to marry. Both of our parents are divorced. My mother and father rarely speak, but his mother and father are actually quite cordial. How do we handle our engagement party?"

You invite everyone and hope they all act like adults. Something to remember—it's not necessary for estranged parents to chitchat. Allow them the comfort of retiring to their neutral corners. If one set of divorced parents gets along, good for them. If the other set is merely being cordial and not causing a scene, that's quite a lot under the circumstances, and they are to be respected for trying.

"Would it be appropriate to have an engagement party for a second marriage?"

The fact that you have both been married before has no bearing on your wish to share your happiness with your friends, so an engagement party is perfectly acceptable for encore weddings. In a more formal time, engagement parties were lavish affairs, and were rarely given when someone was marrying for the second or subsequent time. But now just about anything goes, as long it is done with good taste.

The truth is, because many couples pay for their own encore weddings, quite a few nix the idea of an engagement party and apply the money directly toward the cost of the wedding itself. For those who love a party, however, it's a great way to call their friends together to make that special announcement, and it is also a friendly environment in which to introduce new family members who have not met.

"Is it appropriate for friends to bring gifts to an encore engagement party?"

Gifts are normally not given at encore engagement parties. The reason is that most people getting married for the second or subsequent time are older, working, even settled in a home of their own, and many of the presents friends might offer would not be needed. If a very close friend or relative really wants to give a gift to the bride or groom to be, it is best to present it alone, perhaps at a private dinner party or get-together. Sometimes the bride or groom's family will offer a special gift to their relative's intended, to welcome him or her to the family. These gifts are usually personal, like an engraved money clip for the groom, or jewelry for the bride. If gifts do appear at the encore engagement party, they should not be opened in front of the guests. You don't want to embarrass guests who did not bring a gift.

Length of Time Between Marriages

"What is the proper amount of time to wait before remarrying? My boyfriend and I have both been married before. We would like to set a date for our wedding and announce our engagement as soon as possible."

Legally, the soonest a divorced individual may remarry is the day after the divorce from his or her previous mate is finalized. From an etiquette standpoint, it is best that a divorced person not formally announce his or her engagement until both parties are legally divorced.

If a previous spouse is deceased, good ex-etiquette suggests you wait at least a year before remarrying. There are several reasons for this. First, it demonstrates respect for those who have passed. Years of marriage and possibly raising children together deserve a formal grieving period in which to remember and reflect. Second, the death of a spouse is a very emotional experience, and grief can impair our judgment. The more time you wait between marriages, the less likely the new marriage will be a rebound relationship. Third, as discussed previously, if either of you have kids, the longer you wait, the more time you give the children—whether young or adult children—to adjust. This may take you far past the conventional one-year grieving period. Fourth, waiting shows respect for the deceased's family. They are most likely hurt by their family member's passing, and the thought of you moving on so quickly could appear insensitive to them, which will ultimately color your interactions with them in years to come. Why be concerned about your relationship to ex-relatives? If you have kids, they are your children's aunts, uncles, cousins, and grandparents. You will most likely continue to interact with them, even though your spouse has passed on.

When Your Fiancé Is Not Yet Divorced

Years ago, a person would not become engaged before his or her divorce was final, and technically, that's the way you are supposed to do it today too. But protocol is not as stringent as in years past. If you want to go by the letter of good ex-etiquette, a couple may agree privately to marry, but they should not announce it publicly, and the bride-to-be should not wear an engagement ring in public, until both she and her fiancé are legally divorced from their previous mates. Truthfully, it's just plain tacky to openly advertise how quickly one has moved on, and if there are children involved, especially older children, it may embarrass them that Mom or Dad has moved on so quickly.

Ex-etiquette rule number seven is "Use empathy when problem solving." In other words, put yourself in others' places when looking for the answer to a problem. If it would make *you* feel bad or embarrass you if your estranged husband's girlfriend started wearing an engagement ring before your union was legally terminated, even if you merely heard about it secondhand, don't do it to someone else.

Prenuptial Agreements

A prenuptial agreement is a contract between two people that spells out how assets will be divided if there should be a divorce or death of one of the partners. They became popular at the beginning of the nineteenth century, when there were no laws to protect the wealth of rich families, should an heiress marry a cad of questionable means who wanted her only for her money.

Prenuptial agreements are no longer limited to the extremely wealthy. Since it is now common for both men and women to own property, there are often questions concerning its division should the couple part. There may also be a question of debts accrued. Without a prenuptial agreement, the couple must divvy things up according to the laws of the state in which they live. A prenuptial agreement allows either party to waive the rights specified by the state. It typically lists all the property of both parties and details what each person's property rights will be after they are married.

There are two schools of thought concerning the need for prenuptial agreements. Some people feel that signing a prenuptial agreement undermines trust in a marriage. It assumes there will be a divorce and assigns the division of assets beforehand. Others believe that it offers partners a greater sense of security if there is a huge difference in wealth between the two partners, or if one or both were burned by excessive alimony or an unbalanced division of property in a past divorce.

Whether or not you should enter into a prenuptial agreement depends on your life circumstances. You might want to seriously consider it in any of the following cases:

- you have children from a previous marriage and want to make sure they inherit specific property
- you own a business or are involved in a family company
- you each have significant assets (or one of you has considerably more than the other)
- you are concerned about your future spouse's significant debt

"We don't want to deal with lawyers. Can't we just sign an agreement between ourselves?"

You could, but it may not stand up in court. For something this important, hire an attorney.

"I don't know how to bring up the subject of a prenuptial agreement with my fiancé. I'm afraid it might upset him."

As well it might. It's not uncommon for some to feel the suggestion of a prenup is a sign that they are not trusted, or that there is a question of whether their love is sincere. That shouldn't stop you from mentioning it, though. If you find it difficult to talk about your finances before the marriage, you will find it difficult to discuss them afterward. Nip that one in the bud. Be honest with each other in regard to your assets, and set the stage for an honest, positive relationship in the future.

If you are concerned about your partner's reaction, it might be helpful to find out what he or she thinks about prenups before you suggest one be signed. Look for ways to discuss the subject without personalizing the conversation. For example, do you know anyone who has signed a prenuptial agreement? Using that couple to prompt a conversation, you might say something like, "Honey, Lisa and Mike just had a prenuptial agreement drawn up. What do you think of that?" Leave it open-ended and just listen to your partner's position. That should give you some insight into how to approach the subject when the time is right.

3

Setting the Budget

Although an unlimited budget for a wedding would be nice, most of us do not have that luxury. Add divorce to the scenario, and establishing a budget and setting guidelines for division of expenses becomes even more important. If you're getting married and your parents are divorced, all sorts of questions arise. Who pays for what? Mom? Dad? What if both the bride *and* the groom's parents are divorced? Then how are the expenses divided? Or if you're getting married for a second or subsequent time, do you have to pay for your own wedding?

Even though it's difficult to talk about money, especially when people are at odds, if you determine a wedding budget and agree on a division of expenses, the decisions become far easier to make. It forces you to set priorities and focus on exactly what is important.

Whether this is your first wedding and Mom and Dad are footing the bill, or an encore wedding and you are paying for it yourself, how much things cost will have an impact on your final choices.

To get an idea of what is in store, start by sitting down with pen and paper and asking yourself the following questions:

- What kind of wedding do I envision?
- Do I want a formal wedding with a horse-drawn carriage and fifteen attendants, or a casual ceremony in a friend's backyard? How about a wedding on the beach? Or a ski weekend?
- Do I want to be married in a church?
- Do I want an elaborate reception? A sit-down dinner? A potluck with friends? A live band? A DJ? A limited bar? Champagne? No alcohol?
- Do I want loads of fresh flowers, or can we use the bridesmaids' bouquets as centerpieces? Potted plants? Daisies in Mason jars?

Answering these questions will give you a good idea of where to start. Of course, this is just the beginning. There are far more considerations than these when setting your budget. Just understand that if you choose to have a formal wedding, then you are choosing all the formal trimmings—formal wedding dress, formal wedding site, more guests, larger reception—and all this increases the cost.

A Word to Battling Parents of the Bride or Groom: Find Neutral Ground

So your daughter just announced her engagement to the man of her dreams. You want to throw her a beautiful wedding and will need your ex's financial assistance, yet the two of you can't seem to be together for a minute before an argument starts. What now?

Divorced parents who cannot get along should try to approach their child's wedding planning in a businesslike manner. Think: if this were a business relationship, how would you solve a problem? You would probably set up a meeting with your associate to discuss the matter. That's exactly what you should do with your ex.

Where would you hold a business meeting? Not in front of your home as you battle things out. Not in your living room. Not at a friend's house. A business meeting would be held in a neutral place, like a meeting room at the office, and you would agree upon an agenda before you entered the meeting. That way, you could anticipate problems, consider solutions, and be a problem solver—an asset to the company. Use the same principles for problem solving if you want to be an asset to your family:

1. Find a neutral place. Neither of you should feel that the other has an unfair advantage as you discuss your problem. A public place is best—a restaurant or coffee shop. Feuding parents are less likely to lose their tempers in public.

2. Suggest a time for the meeting. Include a conclusion time. For example, you might say, "How about meeting at 12:30 at Chili's? I have another appointment at 2:00, but that will give us at least an hour. Will that be convenient for you?"

3. If you are thirsty, order a soft drink, not a glass of wine. Alcohol removes inhibitions and easily stirs up bad memories.

4. Don't walk in unprepared. Have suggestions and possible solutions ready.

5. Bring a picture of your child with you and place it right in the middle of the table. If either of you starts to lose your temper, take a good, hard look at the picture. That's why you are there.

6. Leave when you had planned to. If a solution has not been found, make another appointment before you leave. If you and your ex have been making your child your first priority, however, it is likely that you will reach an agreement.

Who Pays for What?

Now that battling family members can approach this issue in a neutral and businesslike way, it's time to consider good ex-etiquette for dividing up wedding expenses.

The Traditional Breakdown of Expenses for First-Time Weddings

The following list provides the traditional breakdown of expenses for a first-time wedding for both the bride and groom. It's a good starting place, and it will help the bride and groom and their families and friends anticipate what is expected of them. The breakdown will be similar, even if the bride has never been married but the groom has. This is only a starting point, however. The high cost of weddings and receptions requires us all to get a little more creative than in years past. Sometimes the family that traditionally finances something is not as well off as the other family, and there is a compromise. Grandparents or other extended family may also help with expenses. Working brides and grooms may feel uncomfortable if they don't contribute. The beauty of getting married today is that you can think outside the box to create the wedding you want.

The Bride's Family
Engagement party, if the couple would like one
Ceremony (including the organist, vocalist, etc.)
Bride's dress and accessories
Flowers for the ceremony and reception, including bridesmaids' and flower girl's bouquets

Transportation for the bridal party from the bride's home to
the ceremony site

Invitations, printing, and mailing

Reception (including food, liquor, music, wedding cake,
reception hall)

Wedding planner, if there is one

Photographer or videographer (groom's family may also pay
for this)

Wedding gift for the couple

The Groom's Family

Rehearsal dinner

Their own travel and hotel accommodations

Their wedding attire

Wedding gift for the couple

The Bride

Groom's ring and gift

Gifts for her attendants, including the flower girl

A party or luncheon for her bridesmaids

Wedding guest book

Thank-you notes (personal stationery)

The Groom

Engagement and wedding ring for the bride

Groom's wedding attire

Wedding gift for the bride

Honeymoon

Marriage license

Officiant (minister, rabbi, or judge performing the ceremony)

Gifts for his attendants, including the ring bearer

Accommodations for attendants, if they are from out of town
(lodging only)

Bride's bouquet

Corsages for mothers, bonusmoms, grandmothers, and
bonusgrandmothers

Boutonnieres for himself, his attendants, fathers, bonusfathers,
grandfathers, and bonusgrandfathers

The Attendants

Their wedding attire (except the ring bearer and flower girl—
their attire is paid for by their parents)

Travel arrangements, should they have to travel to the wedding

Wedding gift for the couple

Showers or bachelor/bachelorette parties

Who Pays for What When Your Parents Are Divorced?

If the bride or groom's parents are divorced, nothing is written in
stone in regard to who pays for what. Logic would dictate that Mom
and Dad split the expenses. But financial standing changes a lot after
divorce. Statistics tell us that men fare better after divorce than
women, and that means most of the responsibility would generally fall
on Dad. However, remarriage may put Dad in a financial bind, or
Mom may have started a successful business. Deciding who pays for
their child's wedding may just be another instance when divorced parents must negotiate their fair share of the responsibility.

> "My parents were divorced four years ago. I feel it was my
> dad's fault, and I admit I still have a lot of anger toward him
> about it. I am not inviting him to my upcoming wedding,
> but I still feel that, as my parent, he should contribute some-
> thing. I've asked him if he can pay for our wedding cake.
> He's acting hurt and balking at paying for the cake."

I don't really know what led up to this horrible state of affairs, but
honestly, if you are being as petty as described, then technically your

father doesn't have to pay for anything. However, that would only perpetuate these bad feelings. I suggest both you and your father refer to ex-etiquette rule number five, "Don't be spiteful," and rule number six, "Don't hold grudges." If your dad can afford the cake, I would advise him to rise above his hurt feelings and say it would be his pleasure to pay for it, and to tell you that he loves you and wishes you only the best. Hopefully, that will lay the groundwork for a better relationship with you in the future. But you should also consider inviting him. Asking anyone, including a father against whom you hold a grudge, to finance something but not attend is mean-spirited and not in good taste. Truthfully, this sounds like a last-ditch effort to let your father see how angry and hurt you are about his decision to leave your mother. Such feelings may be better addressed in a counselor's office than on your wedding day.

> *"I was an only child until my father and mother divorced ten years ago, when I was seventeen. Then my dad remarried and had two more children. I am planning to marry in a year, and he just told me that he cannot finance the wedding I want. I suspect it's because of the cost of his new family. My mom and dad rarely talk, so I know my dad will not try to coordinate financing the wedding with my mom. I'm angry and hurt, and I don't know what to do."*

As an adult, you may intellectually understand budgets and finances, but it may not translate into real life if you are having trouble dealing with favoritism issues now that your father has two more kids. Feelings of favoritism hurt an adult child at thirty just as much as they hurt a child of thirteen. Adults are expected to be able to just deal with it, and when they don't deal with it well, divorced parents are dumbfounded by their "immature" reaction.

If you are facing this as an adult child, it's a sign that it was a problem that was not addressed properly when you were younger—

or when the younger children were born. Take this time to address it now, by considering counseling to sort out your feelings, but also by having a heartfelt conversation with your dad. Allow him to reassure you of his love and concern and to clarify any misconceptions you may have about his choice to have more children. When he tells you he loves you, believe it, because he does. You are his firstborn, and that in itself gives you a unique place in his heart.

Now, let's address the communication issues between your mom and dad. Although you have not mentioned why they divorced, ten years is a long time not to communicate with your child's other parent, and unfortunately you have had to witness this ongoing animosity. Most parents do not understand how their inability to communicate colors their children's memories of growing up. They know their own hurt and pain, and they think they are buffering their children from any pain they might feel as a result of a divorce. But, as you can probably testify, silent animosity between divorced parents can be just as devastating for a child as witnessing a fight. The first step for divorced parents to learn how to problem solve together is not necessarily to learn how to stop the fighting, but to learn to put their child first when making decisions. If they truly do that, the fighting will stop, and that will help shield their children from much of the pain they might feel.

Until your wedding, there really hasn't been a reason for your parents to change the status quo. They have existed for years without talking, and you have accepted it as the way things are. But your upcoming wedding can change things. It's the mark of a new day, and sometimes our children are our greatest teachers. You may have to be the one to set the example this time.

You must accept that your parents may not have the funds to pay for the wedding you want. This may have been the case even if they had never divorced. The easiest way to address finances in cases such as yours is to simply ask each parent for a budget outlining what they can afford, and to make your own decisions about your wedding. This will also eliminate the need for negotiation between less-than-amicable exes.

There is usually ample time before a wedding to lay the ground-work for better communication between family members. Try some of the suggestions listed in chapter 1. They really apply to anyone who has difficulty communicating—not just estranged exes. Hope-fully, when your parents see the effort you are making, they will fol-low suit.

A quick and easy way to get parents to talk to each other is to simply remove yourself from the middle. Saying something as simple as "Please coordinate things with Dad so I know my budget for the band" tells them you expect them to work it out between them. If they drag their feet or balk at the suggestion of working together, just stick to your guns: "I need your help on this one."

> *"My dad is paying for most everything connected to my wed-ding. Yesterday I told him that I would like both him and my bonusdad to walk me down the aisle. He said if that's the way I wanted it, then let my bonusdad foot the bill. I'm heartbroken. I want them both there with me, but my bonus-dad makes half of what my dad makes. He could never afford a wedding like this."*

Your father was hurt by your desire to include your bonusdad in a ritual he regarded as exclusive to him. As a result, his gut reaction was not the best one—and a perfect example of why it's important to consider the ten rules of good ex-etiquette for weddings. Rule number one is "Remember whose wedding it is." It's yours, and it's his place to support your decisions. Your father's hurt feelings are no excuse for him to turn one of the most memorable days of your life into a battleground.

When this sort of ultimatum is made, it is usually done in the hopes that a child will back down. I would be shocked if you chose to acknowledge your bonusdad and as a result your father really followed through on his threat and did not help pay for the wedding. If your dad really thinks it through, hopefully he will see that denying you the wedding you want, based on your bonusdad's involvement, could actually become a self-fulfilling prophecy, putting strain on your father/daughter relationship and setting the stage for an even closer relationship between you and your bonusdad.

When all is said and done, unfortunately, you have been given an ultimatum, and you have no other alternative than to make the decision placed before you. You should appeal to your father's good nature, but if he sticks to his guns, you must make the final decision of whether you want to forgo the big wedding in order to have your bonusdad accompany you down the aisle.

> *"My mom and dad divorced when I was very young, and I was raised by my mom and my bonusdad, whom I regard as my father. Two years ago my biological father unexpectedly reentered my life. Does he have any responsibility to help pay for my wedding?"*

Morally, all parents have the responsibility to support their children, and in a case like this, your biological father should offer to help your mother and bonusdad with the expenses. If they cannot talk freely, to eliminate arguments the most common way to split up such expenses is that Mom and Bonusdad pay for the wedding, and Dad pays for the reception. Of course, this depends on everyone's ability to contribute.

Who Pays for What: Encore Weddings

> *"I have never been married, but my fiancé was married and has two children. Does that mean I have to tone down our*

*wedding, or can I go for the gusto as far as the dress, atten-
dants, and preparations? Even though he's done this before,
I plan on this being it.*"

Traditionally, the bride determines the size and style of the wedding. Even though the groom has been married before, in this case, the bride has not; therefore, the ceremony may be approached as a first wedding. If the bride had been married before, and not the groom, although it is perfectly permissible to have an elaborate fiesta, most encore brides opt for a smaller ceremony—unless there has been a lot of time between weddings, or she had no formal ceremony the first time.

"*I have been married before and have been living with my
current fiancé for three years. He has also been married
before. My parents paid for my first wedding; are they oblig-
ated to pay for another?*"

If both the bride and the groom have been married before, as you both have, or if they are older and firmly established out on their own, then they should pay for the majority of the expenses for their wedding—especially if they have been living together. Your parents may want to host the rehearsal dinner or a private get-together, but it should not be expected.

"*My fiancé and I have both been married before, and have
been living together for almost a year. We plan to pay for our
wedding ourselves but don't have a lot of money. Any suggestions?*"

Guests at your wedding will forget the cake. They will forget the band. But they will not forget how you made them *feel* at your wedding, or how you feel about each other. What do you want to communicate first and foremost to your friends and family at your wedding? A feeling of love. A feeling of devotion. A feeling of commitment. Some of the most extravagant weddings I have attended did not communicate those feelings.

To communicate these feelings on a budget, pay special attention to things such as your vows and the type of music you choose, rather than an elaborate ceremony and reception. You may also want to look into a theme or destination wedding, in which you travel to, say, your favorite ski resort, or even Las Vegas, with a small group of family and friends. See chapter 11 for more information on destination weddings.

4

Getting Organized

ew weddings come off without a hitch, even in those rare families in which there's been no divorce or remarriage for generations. Add multiple partners, bad memories, and hot tempers,
and you are destined for a wedding roller-coaster ride. This chapter
is designed to simplify the planning of the big day by anticipating and
thereby eliminating as many stressful situations as possible.

Who Helps with the Planning?

*"Although my mom and bonusmom get along quite well, I
know there is going to be a problem when planning my wedding. My bonusmom is going to want to be included in all
the planning, and my mom's not going to like it."*

Unless the bride's parent has been out of the picture, and the bride was raised predominantly by the bonusparent, the bonusparent does not participate in the wedding decision making. She can be the official backup, however, and can help the bride, her mother, and the bride's attendants by running errands or, in case of last minute jitters, being close by with a cool cloth and a stable shoulder.

Selecting the Site

The site of your wedding, of course, depends on things like your budget, but also on how formal you have decided your wedding ceremony will be, and how far your guests will have to travel in order to attend the wedding. Many a bride and groom with divorced parents have lamented the stresses of searching for middle ground. One groom about to tie the knot told me he'd been juggling time with both his parents since they divorced when he was twelve years old. The parents lived across the country from each other, and his first impulse was to hold the wedding in between them in Kansas City, even though he and his fiancée both lived in California! Many children of divorce worry about offending or betraying one parent if they "choose" the other's home or city. For example, at first the bride below jumped at the chance to have her wedding at her mother's home, but then anticipated the family fall-out:

> "My mother and stepfather have just moved into a lovely home with a great backyard. My fiancé and I are on a very limited budget—it's a second marriage for both of us, and we are paying for the wedding. I would love to have our wedding at my mother's house, but if I do, I know my father and his wife will not come. They will view it as my picking my mom over them, and that's not it at all. What should I do?"

Shame on your parents for putting this much pressure on you for so many years! Yet it sounds like they will not come to their senses before your big day, so if you truly want both parents at your wedding, look for a neutral place where both will feel comfortable attending. Even though you are working with a limited budget, there are many beautiful options that are free of charge—a neighborhood park with a potluck reception, for example, or a beach with a barbeque reception. You may have to get more creative than you would if you were getting married under your mother's roof, but choosing a neutral place will enable both parents to attend. Ultimately, however, where you hold your wedding is your choice. And if you continue to anticipate your parents' hurt feelings when you make your decisions, things will never be easy. It may be time to take a stand. This means, using the rules of good ex-etiquette, you *politely* inform both parents, their new partners, and extended family of *your* wishes for *your* wedding. Rule number eight, "Be honest and straightforward," comes to mind.

> *"My ex-sister-in-law has remained my best friend even after her brother and I divorced five years ago, and she is still very close to my son. She recently married a man with quite a few 'toys,' one of which is a one-hundred-foot yacht. I'm getting remarried, and she has offered the yacht for my wedding site. I'm really considering it but wonder if it would be in poor taste. "*

Decisions like this really have to be made on an individual basis. The consequences of the breakup may dictate different answers for different people. However, if you are looking for a rule of thumb, you must consider both the consequences of your decision for yourself and the way it might affect others. Ask yourself, what does my decision say to the outside world? What does it say to my ex? What does it say to my former sister-in-law?

Many people stay close to members of their ex's family, and it is understandable. The "former" relative may be their child's grandparent, or aunt, in this case. But other former relatives with whom you are not as close could view your using the yacht as a slap in the face to your ex—especially if your ex is not doing as well as you are now—not to mention that it appears that his sister is openly aligning herself with you. That may not be the intent, but appearances can say something else.

With all this in mind, it will make future interaction with your ex easier, plus cut down on potential gossip within your ex-extended family, if you chose a more neutral place to marry for the second time. This does not prevent your former sister-in-law from being an attendant at your wedding, however. That can be easily explained by the fact that you have remained close after the divorce. But to remarry on a yacht owned by your former sister-in-law's husband stretches the rules of good ex-etiquette pretty tightly—especially if another place that will not offend can easily be found.

Setting the Date

> *"My fiancé and I are both rather casual people, but our families are not. They are very proper and get an attitude easily. To keep disagreements to a minimum, what are some of the things we should take into consideration when picking a date for our wedding?"*

First, and most important, remember that it's *your* wedding. As much as your parents may be financing the affair or offering advice, your wedding ceremony is a symbol of your relationship with your intended and the feelings both of you wish to communicate to your guests. It's not indicative of your parents' relationship or the wedding ceremony they wish they'd had twenty-five years ago. If they are still married and want to plan a wedding that is "them," it may be time to formally renew their vows. If they are divorced, you may want to politely refer them to rule number one of good ex-etiquette for weddings—"Remember whose wedding it is." As much as parents like to run the show, it's not really their show to run. Say that with love and respect.

Second, consider days that are important to your family, and either choose them as potential wedding dates or nix the day altogether. For example, if your grandparents had a long and happy marriage, choosing the same date for your wedding would be a lovely family tribute. On the other hand, suppose the day you would like to marry also happens to be your sister's twenty-first birthday. Another day might be better suited for your nuptials. Don't forget to consider the children in your life when you pick a date. If your fiancé's children do not live with him or her, you may not realize that the date you chose is the day scheduled for soccer finals or a ballet recital. If you plan to have the children in your life in your wedding ceremony, make sure that you confirm that the day you choose works for their schedule, too.

Third, consider how far relatives have to travel to attend the wedding. Are you inviting any very young, older, or disabled relatives who might have difficulty traveling long distances?

Fourth, weather is always a consideration. If you want to lessen the chance of rain or snow on your wedding day, choose a day in a warmer month of the year.

Fifth, planning your wedding on a specific holiday may not be a good choice. The Christmas holidays, for example, are filled with emotion and are often difficult days for families who have faced divorce. The heightened emotion connected to the holiday may overshadow the wedding, and some important relatives may be reluctant to attend. On the other hand, having a lovely wedding that celebrates love and promise for the future at this time of year may just change family members' attitude about the holidays by reminding them to look toward a bright future instead of seething about the past.

"What are 'save the date' cards? And do I need them?"

It's a good idea to send "save the date" cards if you have planned your wedding far in advance or scheduled it during a holiday weekend, or you expect out-of-town guests. This will ensure that they will pencil in your wedding date on their calendar and be sure to attend. Plus, "save the date" cards will help coordinate efforts with Mom's side of the family and Dad's side of the family, not to mention ex-relatives you may want to invite but don't see that often.

"Save the date" cards vary in size and shape from formal cards that look like wedding invitations to simple postcards. They can be homemade on the computer or ordered to match your actual invitations.

In addition to offering the date of your wedding, you may want to include several other things with your card. Some couples like to send their engagement photo. Others do a little research for their out-of-town guests and include information on flights, rental cars, and hotels. The more creative you can be, the less likely they will end up in the circular file. If you use a postcard format, make sure it is easily distinguishable from junk mail.

Here is a sample of a typical "save the date" card:

We are delighted to announce that on June 20, 2008, in Orlando, Florida, Madeline Louise Smith and Thomas Michael Jones are getting married! We would love for you to join us. Please make sure to save the date.

Sincerely,

Maddie and Tom

Formal invitation to follow

"*I just found out the date we chose for our wedding is just three days different from my fiancé's first wedding date. Is it a good idea to pick a date like this?*"

It's time to grow up and realize you are marrying someone with a past. Do not start out your life together by comparing your new life to his old one. Such comparisons are the death of any relationship. *Your* anniversary is the date *you* choose. Although there may always be subtle reminders that there was a life before, acknowledging *your* marital union as the primary relationship now is important to the longevity of your marriage. There will be far greater things to overcome in your life together than an issue as trivial as this.

Choosing Your Officiant

The officiant usually directs the wedding ceremony and can help you get a picture of how your ceremony will flow. The personality of your wedding officiant is important—he or she creates the feeling of your wedding ceremony and ties each stage of the ceremony together—so pick this person well. Set up interviews with one or more candidates and get to know each one.

Discuss your plans for the ceremony with prospective officiants and gauge whether you are comfortable with their responses. Discuss the types of vows you and your fiancé would like to say to each other—whether they will be conventional or you will write your own. Will you have one ring or a double-ring ceremony? What do you plan to say to each other as you exchange rings? Are you comfortable with the traditional "giving away" of the bride, or would you rather have a different expression, with parents of both bride and groom, or even your children, participating? Don't forget to mention the ways in which you want to thank the family and friends who have gathered, and let the officiant know if you will want family, friends, or children to share in the wedding by participating in the readings or hymns.

In addition to discussing your own plans, it's important to discuss the officiant's role and the words he or she will say as well. Notify the officiant if there is anything you're uncomfortable with. For example, there is one line in the traditional Protestant ceremony that I always remind encore couples to modify: "Who gives this woman in marriage?" This is an appropriate question at a traditional first wedding, when the father usually "gives away" the bride, but it is rare that a father plays the same role at an encore wedding. A more appropriate version might be "Who will support this new family with their love and prayers?" Everyone attending the wedding can answer with a hearty "We do!"

One thing to keep in mind is that some faiths or officiants may not be sensitive to divorce and remarriage and may frown upon various rituals that integrate children from previous relationships or stepparents into the ceremony (for example, lighting a unity candle, which is discussed in chapter 9, or having both your dad and your bonus-dad walk you down the aisle). Some officiants will not perform a marriage ceremony at all if either the bride or the groom has been married before. Make sure that the clergyperson is comfortable with your situation and your plans for the ceremony.

> "*I am Jewish, and my fiancé was brought up Methodist. For our sake and the sake of our kids, we'd like both faiths honored in our ceremony. Will we have trouble finding someone to perform the ceremony?*"

Incorporating aspects of both faiths into the ceremony, especially if there are children involved, is an excellent way to demonstrate tolerance and respect for each individual family member's beliefs and to set the stage for the family's future together. Although it sounds nice to have "co-officiants"—one from each faith—in some areas of the country only one officiant can sign the legal paperwork. Check to see what the laws are in the state in which you are marrying. Even if co-officiants are not allowed, if it is agreeable to both officiants, you might be able to make it look like they are both performing the ceremony, even though legally only one will sign and send in the paperwork.

Choosing Your Vows

One of the most difficult decisions a couple about to marry has to make is choosing the vows they will say during their wedding ceremony. Most look for something poignant and meaningful, a heartfelt expression of how they feel now that they have found someone who renews their faith in love, relationships, and "until death us do part."

One way to ensure that your wedding vows are truly special is to write them yourself. Your partner and you are the only ones who know how you feel about love, commitment, and each other. If you decide to write your own vows, be aware that there are things that legally must be included. Your officiant can give you that information. If you are having a religious ceremony, check with the clergyperson to see if there are any standardized words of faith you might use.

Next, sit down with your partner and make a list of what you would both like to say to each other, your families, and your friends about your relationship and future life together. If you need help finding just the right words, there are many books and Web sites (see Resources) that offer help. Feel free to select different portions of various vows and fine-tune them to suit your own needs. Adult children of divorce sometimes pay special attention to their feelings about commitment, trust, and family, while many encore couples look for vows that specifically mention their children and what they envision for their collective life together. Below are some suggestions encore couples can use as a starting point.

_____, *I choose you as the person with whom I will spend my life. I take you, with all your faults and your strengths, as I offer myself to you with my faults and my strengths. I will trust in you, and I will keep your confidences. I will help you when you need help, and will turn to you when*

I am in need. I will care for all of our children and offer them a strong and loving home. Before these witnesses I pledge to love and care for you and our family as long as I live.

or

_____, I promise to be a good and faithful husband/wife to you, and a patient and loving parent figure to [children's names]. I promise to care for them and provide for them as my own. I promise to be their strength and their emotional support, and always hold them dear. I promise to respect this new family and to do everything in my power to make it be a safe haven for each of us.

or

I, _____, choose you, _____, and our children, _____, to be my family. I promise to honor and respect all of you, and to make our home a sanctuary where trust, love, and laughter abound. I make these promises with all my heart and soul, and vow to honor them all the days of my life.

The children can repeat a variation of the above, either separately or together, or the person performing the ceremony can ask the children the following questions:

Officiant: *And now, [children's names], do you promise to care for _____ as your bonusparent?*

Children: *We do.*

Officiant: *To treat him/her with respect as a member of your new bonusfamily, and know that he/she cares for you as one of his/her own?*

Children: *We do.*

Officiant: *Do you promise to be an active member of this new family with the understanding that your mother/father and _____ understand the importance of both of your families, your new bonusfamily, and your other family with your father/ mother, and do not wish you to choose one over the other, but to love and be loved by both?*

Children: *We do.*

It's always nice to personalize your vows in some way, especially if it can add a little humor to the ceremony. For example, I have heard such things said as, "I promise to occasionally share the remote control." Or, "I promise to split the difference when setting the thermostat." Or, "I promise to do the dishes on Tuesday nights if you do them on Thursday nights."

Flowers

For first-time weddings, the bride and groom's families most often share the cost of flowers, with each side responsible for various flower arrangements. Traditional flower expenses are divided as follows:

Bride's Family
Flowers used at the wedding site and at the reception
Bouquets for attendants
Extra corsages for friends or honored guests

Groom

Bride's bouquet

Bride's corsage if she has a going-away outfit

Corsages for the mother of the bride, mother of the groom,
grandmothers

Boutonnieres for the groom, best man and groomsmen,
fathers, and ushers

Encore brides and grooms often pay for their own flower arrangements, which are typically less extravagant than for first-time weddings. Before you contact a florist, do as much research as you can. Have you seen an arrangement in the past that you really liked? Do you remember the types of flowers used? Do some Internet surfing or peruse magazines to find pictures of what you envision that you can share with your florist.

Here are some tips for brides and grooms looking to cut costs on flowers:

- Choose flowers that are in season and locally grown. If you use flowers that are out of season or must be flown in from some exotic location, anticipate higher costs.
- Use flowers only where they are needed. Most churches have a lovely ambiance all their own and need very few flower decorations. In that case, use the majority of your flower budget to decorate the reception site.
- Place an empty vase with water at each bridesmaid's reception table setting. Order hand-tied bridesmaid bouquets with free-hanging stems and use the bridesmaids' bouquets as the centerpieces at the reception. If the bouquets are made of silk flowers, place in dry vases.
- Use fruit to create an impressive centerpiece.
- Use votive candles and flower petals or confetti scattered on tables.

- Use potted plants or potted orchids purchased at your local super-market as centerpieces.
- Flower arrangements and flower costs can truly impact the cost of your wedding, and this is one instance in which hiring a wedding planner can really help. He or she will know where to get deals on flowers and can also make suggestions as to the size of the arrangements and where they should be placed.

"My fiancé's parents are divorced, and both have remarried recently. That means my fiancé has a stepmother whom he does not know very well. We plan to give flowers to the mother and grandmother of the bride and groom. But since we are on a very strict budget, are we required to give flowers to stepmothers and stepgrandmothers as well?"

You are not "required" to give flowers to anyone, really. Flowers are offered to loved ones as a gracious gesture of appreciation, love, and respect. My suggestion is to find the money, even if budgets are tight. Although your fiancé does not know his stepmother well now, hopefully that is only temporary. Excluding the stepmother at a family function, especially a function that expresses love and acceptance, will not promote future family unity. It's just plain not good ex-etiquette.

Now, what about the stepgrandmother? Again, flowers are a small way to include her and make her feel welcomed. My suggestion is to have different bouquets or corsages made up—make sure they are not the same, but not *radically* different—for each of the women in question. It's best not to single out steprelatives by offering them a lesser corsage or token at the wedding. Better to give biological relatives (mother and father of the bride and groom, for example) special responsibilities that will alert guests to their status.

Photography and Video

Encore wedding couples paying for their own wedding may try to cut expenses by hiring a cheap photographer. This can be a big mistake; experienced wedding photographers are rarely inexpensive. I'm not suggesting you must pay top dollar for a photographer, but at least do your homework and make sure you're finding the best photographer within your budget. Below are some tips for ensuring you end up with pictures you'll treasure for a lifetime, no matter what you spend.

- When interviewing photographers and videographers, ask to see examples of their work. Most photographers and videographers have a distinct style. That style is consistent from wedding to wedding and likely will not change for your wedding. If you don't see anything you like, that photographer is not the one for you.

- When viewing the sample books or sample videos, if you like a particular effect, camera angle, or location, point it out and be specific. Say, "I want something like this." Now the photographer understands what you are expecting.

- Ask if the photographer or videographer has ever taken pictures at the ceremony or reception site you have chosen, and if he or she has, ask to see examples.

- Photographers work in different ways, so make sure you understand your particular contract. Many photographers contract for a specific amount of time. If the reception runs long, they will either leave when their contracted time is up or charge you a fee for running longer than expected. Others contract for a set amount of film. Some charge for proofs; others do not. Some like to shoot the wedding party before the ceremony, some after.

- Make a checklist before the ceremony so the photographer can keep an accurate record of pictures he or she has taken. Make sure you don't list just people, but groupings of people as well, such as, "Uncle Tom, Aunt Mary, Grandma Sherry, and bride."

Remember, your photographer will not know who all the players are. You will be busy, so delegate a close friend or relative to point out important people or groups of people to your photographer so you are assured of getting the pictures you want.

Budget-Cutting Tips

There are lots of alternatives to expensive, professional wedding photographers for those on a tight budget. One great way to reduce photo costs is to look for a college student who is just starting out as a professional photographer. Students are often far less expensive and more creative than the conventional wedding photographer. Call a local college and ask the instructor for suggestions. If you decide to hire a student, it is especially important to look at examples of his or her work!

Another way to cut photography costs is to hire a photographer for only the formal shots of the ceremony and wedding party and ask a friend or family member who is a good amateur photographer to shoot the reception. Most of the shots at the reception will be casual, fun shots of people celebrating, which is easy to capture with today's digital point-and-shoot cameras. You can also purchase disposable digital or film cameras and place them on every table so that guests can take photos. It's fun for guests, and it can result in some of the most fun, candid shots of the event.

Where to Position Bonusfamily Members

One of the trickiest issues surrounding wedding day photos when combining families is knowing how to properly position bonusfamily members. The key is to position people so that the viewer can most easily understand to whom everyone is related.

For the encore couple with kids, place the wedding couple near the middle, the children of the husband on their father's side, the children of the mother on their mother's side. If the couple has already had children together, those children are placed between the married couple. Now the viewer can look at the picture and understand that the children or relatives on one side originated with the husband, the children and relatives on the other side originated with the wife, and the children placed between the couple are the couple's children.

The diagrams below should give you some assistance.

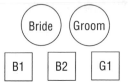

B1 and B2 are the bride's children, and G1 is the groom's child.

If the bride and groom have a child together, the arrangement would then look like this:

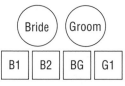

BG is the child the bride and groom have together.

As family members are added to the picture, they should stand on the side of their biological relative.

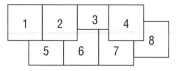

1. Bride's bonusmother
2. Bride's father
3. Bride
4. Groom
5. Bride's child #1
6. Bride's child #2
7. Bride and groom's child
8. Groom's child #1

For adult children of divorce, bonusfamily pictures can be tricky too, as this bride illustrates:

"My mom and dad are divorced and have both remarried. Everyone gets along OK, although there are times when it

gets rather tense. Where does everyone stand? And is it appropriate to take one picture for our wedding album of just us and my parents, without their new spouses? ”

I'll address your second questions first. This might be appropriate if, first, no one is offended, and second, you ensure the photographer takes another picture of them *with* their new spouse. Remember, the ones who might be the most offended by the suggestion of your parents taking a picture together are their new spouses. They think of their husband or wife as their partner and lover first, not as your parent. So to them, you are asking their husband or wife to take a picture with a former lover. But to you, you just want a picture of Mom and Dad. You can get that if everyone can act like adults while the camera is focusing.

There are three ways you can position your divorced parents. One, you can put them both on your side and remind them that it's just a picture, and they are doing it for you—ex-etiquette rule number one: "Remember whose wedding it is." Second, you could suggest that the photographer get creative and seat one of them, perhaps on a chair or step, to avoid everyone crowding in all together for the "happy family" shot. Finally, you might consider forgoing the "parents of the bride or groom" shot and position siblings or grandchildren in between your parents.

There may be a time when the bride and groom both have divorced parents and want a picture of all the parent figures in one picture for the wedding album. In this case, divorced parents are just going to have to stand near each other, perhaps buffered by their new spouses.

If divorced parents are so estranged that it is difficult to be in the same picture together, don't attempt it. Take separate pictures.

Choosing Music and a Soloist

Music plays a major role in most wedding services. It sets the mood and has the power to convey the couple's feelings about their union to those attending the ceremony. It is, therefore, appropriate for you to give careful thought to music in planning your wedding. ·

Most of the couples with whom I have worked feel that their encore relationship is a gift—another chance at love—and if they secretly feel that they contributed to the demise of their previous relationship, a chance for them to do it right this time. As a result, they agonize over the music that will be played during the ceremony, because it is so important to them to convey their feelings of promise and commitment.

When considering music for your ceremony, think beyond just cool songs you like. Look for music that:

- supports the overall focus, theme, and mood of the ceremony
- expresses your faith in the relationship and your joy for the future
- promotes a calm, relaxed feeling

If you are getting married in a church, your organist/pianist can be an important resource for appropriate music, especially if you are not all that musically inclined. Ask him or her for help in planning. Another option might be to use the church choir. Check with the church choir director to see if it is possible. Acoustic folk singers or a string quartet are other options.

The easiest way to find prospective soloists is by word of mouth. Your wedding planner, should you use one, will know of soloists in the area. Representatives of the church or site where you choose to marry will also probably have a list of soloists they can recommend. Local voice instructors may also have students who would make lovely wedding soloists. Make sure you listen to the soloist before you hire him or her and be clear about how much he or she charges. Of course, the soloist will attend the wedding rehearsal and rehearsal dinner.

You may also come from a musically inclined family, in which case a family member can sing in the ceremony. One of the sweetest musical choices I have encountered was when one of the children of the marrying couple sang a solo with a children's choir.

Wedding Ceremony Programs

A wedding program is not required, but if you have the time and resources, it's a great way to add a personal touch to your ceremony. It includes the name of everyone who participates in the ceremony and his or her relationship to the bride and/or groom. Wedding programs are particularly helpful for encore weddings, so that guests who may not know both sides of the family will understand who everybody is.

The following items could be included in the wedding ceremony program:

- the time, date, and place of the ceremony, and the name of your officiant
- the order of events
- the names of all of the members of the wedding party, with explanations of who they are (for example, "John Miller, age ten, son of groom"; "Louise Van der Smoot, bride's best friend since college")
- the titles of any music played and a list of special readings—be sure to include the names of any musicians, soloists, or readers
- a special "thank you" to parents, grandparents, and/or children
- a wish for the future of your new family
- a special message from the bride and groom to their wedding guests
- explanations of any special religious or ethnic wedding traditions that will be part of your ceremony, such as the Hindu *datar* or the unity candle rituals
- your vows, if you would like to share them with your guests

Here is an example of a very simple program for a wedding in which the bride has divorced parents:

The Marriage Ceremony Uniting
Sara Anne Morrison
and
Kenneth Michael Miller

on Saturday, July 21, 2007
at two o'clock in the afternoon
Christian Country Church
Santa Barbara, California

Prelude
Seating of Grandparents and Mothers
"OUR HOUSE" BY CROSBY, STILLS, AND NASH

Attendants' Processional
"CANON IN D MAJOR" BY PACHELBEL

Bride's Processional

"BRIDAL CHORUS" BY RICHARD WAGNER

Greeting
OFFICIANT'S NAME

Unity Candle—Parent's Lighting
"PARENT'S PRAYER (LET GO OF TWO)" BY GREG DAVIS

Scripture Reading—I Corinthians 12
OFFICIANT'S NAME

Exchanging of Vows and Giving of Rings
OFFICIANT'S NAME

Unity Candle—Bride and Groom
OFFICIANT'S NAME

Solo or Prayer
OFFICIANT'S NAME

Announcement of Marriage
OFFICIANT'S NAME

Presentation of Husband and Wife
OFFICIANT'S NAME

Recessional
"WEDDING MARCH" BY MENDELSSOHN

The Wedding Party

Parents
Mr. and Mrs. Braden Stephenson
Mr. and Mrs. Doug Morrison
Mr. and Mrs. Michael Miller

Grandmother of the Bride
Mrs. Tillie Brown

Grandparents of the Groom
Dr. and Mrs. George C. Miller

Bridesmaids
Miss Lucy Morrison, bride's sister
Miss Samantha Smith, friend of bride
Miss Louise Bartell, friend of bride

Groomsmen
Mr. Michael Stephenson, bride's bonusbrother
Mr. Justin Taylor, bride's cousin
Mr. Joseph Miller, groom's brother
Mr. Richard Miller, groom's brother

Flower Girl
Miss Lisa Morrison, bride's niece

Ring Bearer
Mr. Bobbie Washington, groom's cousin

Officiating Minister
Pastor Larry Adams

Soloist
Miss Harleigh Ford

Pianist
Mrs. Carol Rice

Wedding Director
Mrs. Joyce Bart, bride's aunt

Guestbook Attendant
Louise Morrison, bride's bonusmother

5

Attendants and Attire

The "wedding party" traditionally consists of the bride and groom and their attendants. These can include the maid of honor or matron of honor, bridesmaids, junior bridesmaids, flower girl, best man, groomsmen (ushers), junior groomsman (usher), and ring bearer. Choosing your wedding party and what all of you will wear is one of the major sticklers associated with ex-etiquette for weddings. If your parents have divorced and remarried, you may have siblings, half-siblings, and bonussiblings. Do you ask everyone to be an attendant? What if they are ten years older or younger than you? Won't they seem out of place? And, if it's an encore marriage, and one or both of you have kids, should they be attendants? This chapter will offer help in navigating these often treacherous waters.

Attendants

Selecting the size and makeup of the wedding party is never an easy task, especially if you have a large extended family that includes relatives past and present, plus close friends who feel like family. There can also be added pressure from parents and extended family to include siblings from all marriages. Being asked to be an attendant is the ultimate compliment, but those who have been chosen must understand that with the honor come specific duties that are quite important and time consuming, especially for the best man and maid of honor. These two honored attendants serve as the bride and groom's right hands and troubleshoot problems when the bride or groom is too busy or too overwhelmed to make a decision. They fill in in a pinch—and there are lots of pinches when planning a wedding—so make sure the people you choose for these posts are up to the task.

"My fiancé and I have both been married before, and we just want a small wedding. Must we have attendants?"

You don't need to have attendants if you want a smaller wedding, but you do need to have someone formally sign your marriage certificate as a witness—that's one of the main responsibilities of a best man and a maid of honor. (However, if you elope, the justice of the peace will have someone close by who can act as a witness.)

"Although I have never been married, my fiancé has been married twice before. We have still decided on a formal wedding. Is there a rule about the number of attendants we ask to be in the wedding?"

The size and formality of the wedding is usually based on whether the bride has been married before or has children from a previous relationship. It seems a little sexist by today's standards, but that has always been the criterion used. Therefore, this bride can approach her wedding as the first-time bride that she is, even though her fiancé has been married before. For a first marriage, a bride may ask as many as four to six bridesmaids to be her attendant.

Encore brides, on the other hand, most often choose two or three female attendants, and then the groom matches that number.

Bonusfamily as Attendants

"*My fiancé and I are having a very small second wedding. We agreed to have only two attendants. I have already chosen my best man. I don't know whom to choose for my second atten-dant—my brother-in-law or my bonusbrother.*"

The rules of good ex-etiquette do not provide a definitive answer to this question. It is truly up to the bride or groom. A possible solution is to ask one to be a groomsman and walk in the procession and the other to be an usher and help seat guests.

"*I would like both my sister and my stepsister to be my atten-dants, but they are very jealous of each other and do not get along. What do I do?*"

You use good ex-etiquette and invite both. However, it's not the bride's job to play referee at her own wedding. Explain beforehand to both of them that you have asked the other, and ask if either will have a problem supporting you—not appearing with the person they don't like, but *supporting you*. It is then up to them to accept or decline. Hopefully, when faced with this question, stated in this way, they will allow their love for you to rule over their jealousy of each other. If they both decide to attend, then they are acknowledging that they will act like adults in public.

"*I grew up with three sisters and a stepsister. I do not want my stepsister as an attendant, but my mother is putting a lot of pressure on me. How do I handle it?*"

While you're free to choose some, all, or none of your siblings as attendants, good etiquette demands that you not single out your bonussiblings for exclusion simply because they are bonussiblings. To make the right decision here, ask yourself what kind of statement you are making if you don't include your stepsister in your bridal party. What you're making clear to her, your mother, your bonusdad, and the outside world is that you don't like her. What is the point? Singling out any sibling, bio or bonus, when all siblings were raised together is hurtful and mean-spirited. You may never be friends with your stepsister, but for the sake of future generations, it's important to be as kind as you can to each other—and that means including her as your attendant.

"Do I need to ask my fiancé's bonussister to be a bridesmaid? Should my fiancé invite my bonusbrother to be a groomsman?"

If the bride and groom were raised with their bonussiblings, then bonussiblings should be included as attendants. If they lived on the East Coast, you lived on the West Coast, and you know about each other but rarely socialize except when someone gets married, there is no need to include them as attendants. Seat them as honored guests at the ceremony.

If you would like to include bonussiblings in the ceremony, but not as attendants, you might want to ask them to escort your grandparents to their seats, pass out the wedding programs, do a reading during the ceremony, or oversee the guest book. Make sure to give them boutonnieres or corsages to wear to designate that they are honored guests.

"I would like my stepdaughter-to-be to be a bridesmaid, but she is only twelve years old. Is that too young?"

Probably. Bridesmaids and groomsmen or ushers are usually best friends or cherished relatives of the bride and groom. Their age is not typically a determining factor, unless they are so young that they cannot fulfill the responsibilities associated with being chosen as an attendant. Then they should be relegated to junior status. Junior bridesmaids and ushers are between eight and fourteen years old and walk in the processional, but they have no other formal responsibilities in terms of the ceremony. They do attend the rehearsal dinner, however, and should be available for all wedding photos or videos. Asking someone to be a "junior" is a way of expressing love and respect for a young friend or relative without hampering him or her with "adult" responsibilities.

> *"My husband and I have been married for seventeen years, and we have a twelve-year-old daughter. My husband has two older daughters from a previous marriage, the elder of whom is getting married in November. Understandably, she is having her sister as chief bridesmaid and a close friend as her maid of honor. We had hoped she might also include her younger half-sister (our daughter) in the bridal party, but she hasn't asked her, even though they get along very well. We're not sure why she hasn't asked her, or what we should do about it. Should we speak with her?"*

Asking the bride to include your younger daughter as an attendant would be inappropriate. If the two young women are as close as is mentioned, there's probably a good reason why the younger sibling was not asked. Questioning the bride's choice would certainly put her on the spot—and that's not good ex-etiquette.

There are several reasons why your bonusdaughter may not have asked her younger half-sister to be her attendant. First, consider your young daughter's age. At twelve, she is considerably younger than the bridal party and could be looked upon as "just a little kid." If the bride has only two attendants, she has definitely decided to keep the wedding small, and this may be another reason for the choice. Her sister and best friend are the most logical choices. The youngest daughter could participate as a junior bridesmaid; however, few brides add junior bridesmaids to the bridal party unless there are younger groomsmen on the list as well. Adding another attendant may simply not fit the bride's vision of her wedding.

I am now going to address something rather painful, but part of life concerning extended family after divorce. Another possibility is that the mother of the bride may not view your younger daughter as part of her family and incorrectly thinks of her as having no relation to her daughter. If that is true, she could be playing down the necessity of including the younger sibling in the wedding party and interfering with the bonding between the two siblings. This may be something your husband will want to take up with his first wife, but you should not get involved.

There are other things your young daughter can do at her sister's wedding. She can be seated as an honored guest and wear a beautiful corsage. She can greet guests, or she can oversee the guest book. Any of these will make her feel like she is part of the festivities and of help to the bride.

Realize, too, that sometimes as parents we hurt for our children and want to run defense for them when they don't even realize that there is a problem. This may be the situation here. As it is, your young daughter will be invited to the ceremony and will have an excuse to get dressed up. You can ask the photographer to take a picture of her with the bride and groom for a special keepsake. At twelve years old, that may be all she wants.

"My bonusmom has never tried to take my mom's place—she's always just tried to be a pal. And through the years, that's exactly what she has become, my best pal. She is so excited that I am getting married, and I would love to ask her to be my matron of honor, but I think it would break my mother's heart."

Rarely do I hear from families where the bonusparent has done too good of a job! But as you can see, there may be some repercussions from even the best of circumstances. You see, biological moms would like to think that *they* are their daughter's best friend. If a mother finds that her daughter actually considers her stepmother to be her best friend, it can lead to jealousy and hurt feelings.

Knowing this, simply explain to your bonusmom that you feel she is your best friend, but that you fear choosing her to be the matron of honor would hurt your mother. Then choose either your sister or another good friend as your matron of honor. If you're as close to your bonusmom as you say you are, she'll understand. You might want to give her a little wink and say, "I have something special in mind for you." Suggestions for a special tribute to your bonusparent during the ceremony or at the reception can be found in chapter 9.

> *"I would like to have my fiancé's eight-year-old daughter as my maid of honor, and my fiancé would like my ten-year-old to be his best man. Is this good ex-etiquette?"*

Actually, it's a lovely gesture, and it's important to include your children in the wedding ceremony, but if you are having an elaborate ceremony, asking them to be the best man or your maid of honor may not be the place for that. These two attendants have specific duties, and asking a young child to serve in the capacity of maid of honor or best man may just double your work as you fill in where he or she can't. For example, if, as in this case, the maid of honor is too young to drive, an overstressed bride and groom may find themselves doing twice as much, leaving them exhausted and short-tempered.

Also, it is rare that children, even teenagers, understand the compliment you are trying to give them by asking them to be maid of honor or best man. In my opinion, it is better to assign those duties to your best friend and allow your kids to participate in the wedding by being kids—reciting a poem, lighting the unity candle, or merely standing next to you as the families unite. Other ways to honor your children are discussed in chapter 9.

"My fiancé and I are about to marry after living together for a year. His former wife passed on four years ago when his son was two and his daughter was eight. I get along great with his son, but his daughter shies away from me. I have no children of my own yet. This is my family, and I would like both of the kids to be in the wedding. His daughter refuses."

Your new bonusson was very young when his mother passed away. You are probably the only mother figure he truly remembers at this point. If you are good to him, as it sounds like you are, he's probably crazy about you and wants you and Daddy to marry. Your new bonusdaughter, on the other hand, is another story. She was eight when her mom died. She remembers her and probably misses her very much. Your being around, plus being nice to her, just reminds her how much she misses her mother. You may even have noticed that the nicer you are to her, the more she resents you. She's secretly comparing you two. That's why she keeps you at arm's length. The only thing that will heal this is if she learns to trust you, and at this point, she may not allow herself to do that.

Years ago I worked with a family who was facing this exact problem, and the way the new partner bridged the gap has always stuck with me. One night, after a particularly heated argument which culminated with the dreaded, "You're not my mother!" the bonusmom had a heart-to-heart with her bonusdaughter. She acknowledged that she understood that the child would always have a special place in her heart for her deceased mother. She then asked if the child thought her mother would want her to be lonely or not feel safe. Of course, the child said that, no, her mother would never want her to feel that way. The bonusmom then asked the child if she could look at it as if she was simply helping her mother to take care of her. She presented herself as the deceased mother's partner in raising the child, working alongside her memory, never taking the mother's place, but being a parental figure who now cared for the child because her mother could no longer be with her. That's when the child began to accept the woman's help and affection.

When the child realized she didn't have to choose between her mother and her bonusmother, she began to accept them both. The thing that many people forget in these situations is that the child's allegiance to the deceased parent does not stop because the parent is deceased. A loved one never dies in a child's heart.

The best thing you can do right now is to be patient. Have a heart-to-heart talk with your bonusdaughter, perhaps using the approach I suggested above. Start now, so you will have plenty of time to build a rapport before the ceremony.

Ex-Relatives as Attendants

> "*My ex-sister-in-law is my best friend. I've known her for fourteen years. She introduced me to her brother and refused to take sides during the divorce because she loved us both. She is also my two children's favorite aunt. I am getting married again, and I would like to ask her to be my maid of honor, but by doing this I run the risk of offending not my fiancé, because he knows her very well, but my ex, who hates the fact that his sister and I are still close. But if I don't ask her, I know her feelings will be hurt.*"

Whom you ask to be your attendant is your choice, especially at your encore wedding, where you really can write your own ticket, no matter what the situation. First weddings are often run by the parents of the bride and sometimes don't reflect what the couple really wants. The encore wedding can symbolize the true personality of the two people marrying. The bride and groom can create the feeling *they* want and can communicate their love for each other and for others by the setting they choose, the clothes they wear, the words they select for their vows, the music they play, the food that is served, and the attendants they choose. If your ex-sister-in-law is your best friend, then that's whom you invite to be your maid of honor. That kills one bird—your friend will not be hurt. Now, what to do about the ex?

Former partners often have allegiance and betrayal issues. It's not uncommon for divorced men and women to expect their relatives to sever ties after divorce as a sign of allegiance, and when their relative—especially if it's a close one, like a sister, brother, or parent—wishes to continue the relationship, they feel completely betrayed. As a result, ex-relatives may resort to keeping a continued relationship secret. The ex's sister hasn't done that in this case. She has kept everything on the up and up, and that is using very good ex-etiquette.

Choosing one over the other isn't the issue. Your former husband's ability to deal with the situation rests upon his ability to allow the relationship between you and his sister to continue to exist separately—not necessarily in relation to him. He must accept that his sister loves him, and her allegiance has not wavered. His sister and you have become friends and have formed a bond over the years. Plus, in this case, the ties that bind are not only bonds of friendship; there are children who are related to all. The only relationship that is regarded as "former" or "ex" is the relationship between the two divorced parents. Your ex-husband's sister continues to be his children's aunt even after divorce. And if his sister has children, then you continue to be their aunt.

To ease your ex's mind, his sister and you might make a pact that dishing about him is off limits—and make sure he knows that you have. But other than that, if an ex-relative is your choice as maid of honor or best man, as long as you keep all the relationships separate, start picking out dresses or tuxes.

Attire

The beauty of today's weddings, whether they are first-time or encore, is that a creative couple can take elements of this and elements of that to create the wedding they really want. Formal wedding gowns and tuxedos can be worn at a wedding on the beach, and more casual attire can be worn at a wedding in a church or synagogue. The creative bride may even want to try a different approach to what the attendants wear. Rather than matching color and style, as is most commonly done, why not try matching just the style of the dress and let your attendants choose whatever colors look best on them? Or pick the color the attendants should wear and offer a selection of dresses so that each bridesmaid can choose the one that best matches her body type.

The Bride's Attire

"I had problems with drugs and alcohol, and although I have been married twice before, my past two weddings are just a blur. I have been clean and sober for five years now, and I really want to have a nice wedding as a symbol of my wonderful relationship and new life. We are getting married on the beach in Hawaii, and I would love to wear a conventional white wedding gown, but does that seem silly?"

Gone are the days when a rigid dress code dictates what an encore bride should and shouldn't wear when getting married. White is no longer symbolic of virginity, thank goodness, but of joy. I have found that many times, as in your case, what a bride chooses to wear for her encore wedding is more a symbol of how she feels about the upcoming union at this point in her life than a statement of proper etiquette.

> *"I have been divorced twice, and both times I was married by a justice of the peace in Reno, Nevada. This time I want everything—a church wedding, the white gown. If I do that this time, maybe it will stick, right?"*

Sounds like superstition to me. "If I tap the ground three times and wear my lucky hair band, then this marriage will be a success." Superstition doesn't lay the groundwork for a lasting marriage. Marriages stick when both partners are committed to making it work and have a vision for success in place before they say "I do." So wear what you must, but remember, it's you, not the dress, that seals the deal.

> *"I'm forty years old and marrying for the second time. I was told that long trains and veils are for young brides, but I really want to wear this dress that has a very long train, with a beautiful veil. What do you think—will I look silly?"*

I think this really depends on the bride—whether you can pull it off. I have been to encore weddings where the bride was over forty, wore a conservative, traditional wedding gown, and looked lovely. I have also been to encore weddings where the bride wore a traditional wedding gown and did look out of place, especially when the groom was older, too. As much as this new love of yours makes you feel like an ingenue, you're not, and if you don't watch out, you could look silly.

In these cases, maids of honor should speak up! The maid of honor's job is to be the bride's right hand and honestly advise her. If the bride is planning to wear something inappropriate, it's up to the maid of honor to tactfully make other suggestions.

If you do decide to go this route, you should pay special attention to the veil you choose. Long, flowing veils that hide your face still symbolize virginity or innocence and are traditionally reserved for younger, first-time brides who have never had children. Try a short, off-the-face veil, a hat, or perhaps a tasteful floral headpiece.

"This is my second marriage. Do I even have to wear a wedding gown?"

No. Although some encore brides choose to wear traditional wedding gowns, if money is a consideration, or it's simply not your style, feel free to opt for something that can be worn on other occasions, like a tea-length gown or even a dressy suit. If you are having a casual wedding, you may want to dress even less formally.

"Although I've never been married, I do have a three-year-old son. Somehow a white wedding gown seems a little out of place."

A single mother, or a pregnant bride, for that matter, should feel free to wear white at her wedding, because, as mentioned previously, it no longer symbolizes virginity, but represents joy. Some brides in this situation choose to wear off-white or cream simply because these colors appeal to them more but still offer the feeling of being a princess bride for once in their lives.

Rather than hide the "bump" under long, flowing skirts, today a pregnant bride often openly celebrates the upcoming birth of her child through the style of wedding dress she chooses. High Empire waistlines are comfortable and accentuate the pregnant middle. A pregnant bride should notify the person fitting her dress at the first meeting so that the seamstress can accommodate her growing tummy.

"This is my second wedding and my fiancé's third. He wants to really go for it this time and says he wants me to wear a

'sexy' dress to our wedding. To him, sexy means short. To me, sexy means a little tighter than I might normally wear, and maybe off the shoulder. I keep telling him that brides don't wear miniskirts, but he says I'm just not adventurous. I'm adventurous—I'm marrying him! What should I wear?"

A wedding, first or encore, is a dignified occasion, especially if you are having a religious ceremony. Wedding dresses today are not all poofy and princesslike; many sport flattering lines or come in clingy fabrics that will communicate "sexy" in a tasteful, not sleazy, manner. The miniskirt is for hanging out with friends at the beach or bar and is not really appropriate for a wedding. If he takes it personally, buy a skimpy outfit just for him and model it on your wedding night. It's my bet that will end the disagreement.

Another idea, volunteered by a very creative seamstress who faced a similar problem with one of her clients, was to design a floor-length, satin-lined lace skirt overlay that was held together at the waist with satin ribbon and Velcro. It would look beautiful during the ceremony, and then the skirt could be removed at the reception to reveal a sexy, satinlike spandex minidress. Classy wedding, sexy reception.

Parent and Stepparent Attire

"My mother and stepmother are very competitive, and it really gets me down. One will dye her hair blonde; the other will dye it blonder. One will get a new Cadillac for Christmas; the other will show up with one for Valentine's Day. I'm thinking about secretly buying them the exact same dress to call to their attention how silly they've been all these years. It's been horrible—and I love them both very much."

You describe a problem that has grown out of control—and you have made a suggestion to handle it creatively. If it were any occasion other than your wedding, I would have said "Go for it!" However, there are so many memories associated with your wedding that I'm not sure if you should risk a bad outcome. Although a father and stepfather of a bride would most likely not have a problem wearing very similar attire to her wedding even if they didn't get along, you can bet that mothers and stepmothers would not feel that way.

The mother of the bride takes her dressing cues from the colors and style chosen by the bride. For example, if it's a formal daytime wedding, the mother of the bride would typically wear a long dress with accessories in the color and style of the wedding. The mother of the groom, and stepmothers of the bride and groom, take their cues from the bride's mother. In other words, if the bride's colors are peach and cream, the mother of the bride might choose a tone of darker peach that matches the theme of the wedding. The stepmother of the bride should not wear the exact shade of peach, nor the same dress in a different color. Another color and a complementary style that would blend with the bride's chosen colors would be more appropriate. If the mothers of the bride and groom and the stepmothers of the bride and groom cannot talk to each other to coordinate their dress choices, they should look to the maid of honor for help.

A note to parents and bonusparents: this is not a time to dig in your heels, establish territory, or try to one-up each other. You should set the example for good behavior. For help, refer to the rules of good ex-etiquette for weddings.

Here's a quick reference borrowed from *Ex-Etiquette for Parents*, in which an entire chapter is dedicated to helping biological parents and bonusparents (we call them "counterpartners") get along so that they can coordinate efforts for the benefit of the children in their care:

1. Have a goal for your relationship.
2. You do not have to be friends. Cordial is fine.

3. Don't try to be the children's mother or father. They already have one.
4. Find your niche. Let your counterpartner find his or hers. Then both can offer their best to the children.
5. Develop empathy.
6. Cultivate respect.
7. Formally acknowledge your counterpartner's good work.
8. Don't compare. Don't compete.
9. Learn to ask your counterpartner's opinion.
10. Don't add fuel to the fire.

Adhere to these rules as they apply to your child or bonuschild's wedding, and he or she will be eternally proud of you, and the guests will be in awe. Wouldn't you rather that guests gossip about how well you appeared to get along, rather than how poorly you interacted? Don't kid yourself; they *will* gossip. Make your family proud.

6

Guest List and Invitations

Your wedding invitation does more than merely invite guests to your wedding. As soon as your guests receive it in the mail, the stationery, the color, and the design you've selected let them know if your wedding will be formal or casual, conventional or unconventional. The wording you've chosen tells them if the bride or groom's parents are divorced, or if this is an encore wedding. Your invitation sets the tone of your ceremony and reception.

The guest list is another story. It is supposed to comprise your closest family and friends, but add divorce and remarriage to the mix, and all of a sudden that list gets longer, and invites become questionable. Should we invite Uncle Al's new girlfriend, even though he's not legally divorced from Aunt Alice? And what do you do when Mom invites everyone from her side of the family, and there's no room for Dad's side of the family? All this and more will be discussed in this chapter.

The Guest List and Invitations for Encore Weddings

The guest list for the encore wedding begins with the bride and groom's families, plus mutual friends. But more than with a first wedding, when Mom and Dad may have had some influence over who was invited because they might have foot the bill, the encore wedding is truly the couple's opportunity to celebrate their own good fortune with family and friends. This time, since the bride and groom are most likely paying for the majority of the wedding themselves, the guest list can include anyone they want to invite to join in the festivities.

Inviting an Ex

"My fiancé and I just announced our wedding. We have been living together, and over the years we have become quite cordial with my ex because we co-parent the children. She just assumed she would be invited to our wedding and is asking about our plans. I had no intention of inviting her. How do you handle it when someone assumes they will be invited, but they won't be?"

With someone other than the father or mother of you or your fiancé's children, that's easy. Without an invitation in hand, no one should assume he or she is invited anywhere. When you do run into a situation like this, simply explain that the budget is very tight, and the guest count will be very small. Of course, this excuse will not work if you are planning a large wedding. In those instances, you must weigh whether this friendship is one that you want to continue, because notifying someone that he or she will not be invited is sure to provoke either anger or hurt feelings. If you do not want to upset the individual, hold off as long as possible to see how many regrets you receive; you may be able to fit the guest in.

In your case, when you have a presumptuous ex on hand, it's trickier. If you are all cordial, it means you have cultivated the relationship for a long time, and upsetting him or her could have a lasting effect on all your good work. Hopefully, your relationship has been built on honesty, and in that case, be honest. Simply tell him or her the truth: "Although I value our relationship and do look on you as a friend, I would feel a little uncomfortable with my ex at my wedding. I hope you understand."

There are gestures that you can make that will let an ex know that you value his or her place in the family, but that you don't think it is appropriate that he or she attend. For example, one encore bride told me:

"My husband has twin seven-year-old daughters with his ex-wife who will both serve as flower girls in our wedding. My husband is quite good friends with his ex, and although we did not invite her to the wedding, we asked the wedding photographer to take some special photos of the girls in a lovely setting, and then we gave her the pictures as a special present. It would be unlikely that she would ever have such lovely pictures taken of the girls, and she really appreciated that we thought of her."

"My ex and I are really good friends, and I would like him to attend my wedding. Is that poor ex-etiquette?"

When couples stay in contact with each other after divorce, it is usually for the sake of their children. This relationship may then evolve into a friendship as a result of their mutual interest—their kids. In these cases, if the fiancé doesn't mind, then inviting the ex may be something to consider. However, the basic criterion for making good ex-etiquette decisions when there are children involved is the question "How will this decision affect our kids?" If your ex's attendance would embarrass or confuse them in any way, it may be best to forgo the invitation and invite him to a private family get-together after you return from your honeymoon.

If you do not have children together, then typically there's no need to invite an ex. Continuing a relationship with an ex when there are no children involved may give one partner false hope of reconciliation and prevent him or her from moving on. It may also make a new partner jealous. An exception would be if you continue to travel in the same social circles and remain codial, or a strong friendship has developed between your ex and your child, even though they are not related, as in the example below:

> *"My second husband, John, and I are divorced, and I'm getting remarried. Although we never had kids together, he is the only father my son from my first marriage has known, and he is also good friends with my fiancé. My son and my fiancé would both like John to attend the wedding. I'm OK with it, but my mother will never forgive how he treated me (he was unfaithful), and she has threatened to make a scene if he attends my wedding."*

The guest list is up to you, especially if your son is asking you to invite this man who acted as a father figure, and your fiancé has developed a friendship with him and feels comfortable inviting him. Your mom is reacting from a place of pain—she hurt for you when your ex left. It will help you make your decision if you point out a few things to your mother in a tactful and loving way.

First, if the stepparent becomes close to the child, it can be detrimental to the child's welfare to cut off contact. It is in the best interest of a child whose formative years were spent with a stepparent to allow the child to remain in contact with that stepparent if the child chooses. Your son looks to your ex as a source of security, and if your ex is friendly with your fiancé, then it may add to his security if your ex is there.

There is one important concern, however: your son must also bond with your fiancé, and your ex's presence at the wedding could interfere with your son's ability to bond with your new husband, become an active member of your new family, and wholeheartedly participate in the ceremony. You may decide not to invite your ex, not because you are afraid your mom will come unglued, but because it may be in the best interest of your child.

Second, remind your mother that the first rule of good ex-etiquette for weddings is "Remember whose wedding it is." It's yours, not hers, and what you really need from her at this time is her support of your effort to once again make a go of it, not a public reprimand of an ex from whom you have moved on. Remind her that she is stuck in the hurt, but you are not, and if she really wants to support you, she will enthusiastically embrace your effort to start a new life. If, after this little lecture, she is still looking for revenge, remind her that the sweetest revenge is always to successfully move on and have a happy life—and that's exactly what you have done. And, with a hug, invite her to do the same.

Inviting Ex-Relatives

"I've remained close to my in-laws, even though their daughter ran off and left me with three children to raise alone. I am now remarrying. Should I invite my ex-in-laws to the wedding?"

Ex-in-laws are rarely invited to a second marriage if the first marriage ended in divorce, especially if it was a messy one. Let's examine why. One of the reasons one uses good ex-etiquette, aside from a desire to do what is best for the kids, is to eliminate the possibility of gossip. Most attending the wedding will know the particulars of why the previous marriage broke up, even if the reason that was given was merely "She ran off with that sailor in Hawaii." No matter how close her parents are with her ex, it is unlikely that they will want to go to a gathering where people know full well that their child behaved badly.

The exception is when everyone involved has remained friendly enough that the children would think it strange that their relatives were not included on the guest list. The gauge is the comfort level of all concerned. When in doubt, it can easily be explained to children that "I also love Grandma and Grandpa very much, but they are not coming to the wedding." If said in that manner, using the phrase "not coming," rather than "not invited," children are less likely to become concerned that Mom or Dad no longer cares for their grandma or grandpa.

"I was married for nine years to a wonderful man who gave me nothing but happiness. Sadly, he was killed in a plane crash five years ago. Presently I am in a great relationship, and we plan to marry next year. I am very close to my ex-in-laws, even closer than I am to my own parents, and I know they will share in my joy of finding someone else with whom to share my future. Is it appropriate to invite them?"

Yes, in a case like this, former in-laws may be invited. This is especially true if you and your first husband had children together. This may be difficult for your new partner to understand until he really considers the fact that your in-laws are his new bonuschildren's grandparents. It is the responsibility of new bonusparents to continue to support an existing relationship between grandparent and grandchild, or aunt or uncle and niece. That's what it means to put the children first.

If you decide to invite the ex-in-laws, you may want to honor them by seating them in the third row on the bride's side at the ceremony. Or if you want to invite them but not call special attention to them being there, simply seat them as regular guests.

If you decide not to invite the ex-in-laws, I suggest you set aside time for a personal phone call to them. Explain your continued affection for them, the awkwardness of the situation, and your decision. If you are as close as you say, they will likely understand and hold no grudge. As a way to smooth things over, suggest a private dinner at which you can all meet, talk, and relax.

Inviting Kids

"My son is invited to my wedding, but he lives with my ex-wife in another state. Should I send him a formal invitation?"

If you and your ex do not get along, then sending a formal invitation to her home might appear like you are flaunting your new marriage, and that's poor ex-etiquette. However, it's important to make sure that your son knows that he is invited, welcome, and that you love him. Your best bet would be to discuss your remarriage and wedding plans with your son by phone or through a letter (e-mail seems rather impersonal), and forgo sending a formal invitation. Just remember that your ex-wife should be notified at some point so that the news of your new marriage does not come from your son. That could be perceived as just more fuel for the fire.

If you and your ex are on friendly terms, however, and support each other's desire to remarry, and if you are confident that your ex-wife will not badmouth or undermine you in front of your son when the invite arrives, then sending an invitation to your child in the mail is appropriate. He will probably like to save it as a keepsake.

"I am getting married next month, and I want my kids to be there, but they will be at my ex's house that day, and we barely talk. How do I handle the logistics?"

If you have laid the proper groundwork, even the most estranged divorced parents should not be surprised when you announce your wedding plans and the fact that your kids will be invited. If you cannot speak to your ex in person, a note advising him or her of your plans and when you expect to pick up the children will suffice.

Make sure the wedding is planned on a weekend that is already scheduled for visitation. Asking an uncooperative ex to rearrange his or her plans so the kids can attend your wedding will most likely get a resounding "No!" If the ex refuses to let the children participate on a day stipulated for visitation, you have recourse in the courts—he or she is preventing visitation, and that is illegal. If your ex becomes threatening and you fear an altercation, you may have to look to the law for assistance in advance of the wedding in the form of a restraining order.

> *"I would like to formally invite my sister's bonuschildren to my wedding. They are between the ages of eleven and thirteen. Do I need to send them separate invitations, or may I just tell their parents they are invited?"*

Of course you can tell their parents, but if you are looking for "proper," an invitation should be issued to all children over the age of ten or eleven whom you wish to invite. You may send one invitation to all the children in one family, if you like. In that case, the inner envelope is addressed to the children—for example, "Michael and Billy."

> *"This is my second marriage, and most of my friends have kids. I know some of my friends will want to bring their children to our wedding, but we are on a very strict budget; plus, it's a candlelight ceremony at midnight on New Year's Eve. I just don't think kids are appropriate. How do I tactfully tell them not to bring their children?"*

The time of your ceremony should be a good enough indicator to your guests that children are not invited. Of course, there may be some really dense parents who feel it is appropriate to drag their children out of bed to attend a midnight wedding. If you want to be polite, and if you or your attendants are asked if children are invited, simply say, "Gee, midnight is terribly late for children, isn't it?"

If it's an afternoon wedding, it might not be as obvious that children are not invited. Another way to offer a hint to people whom you fear will bring their kids is to *not* include the words "number attending _____" on the reply card, and to be sure to list the name of each adult invited on the envelopes. This is a good way to indicate that the invitation is open only to the people to whom it is addressed, not the entire family. Children should be left at home if either their names or "and family" are not included on the invitation. There is one exception—if the child is a newborn and the mother is nursing. As a courtesy, the nursing mother should sit near an *outside* aisle so that she can excuse herself quickly if the child begins to cry. Parents should make child-care arrangements for toddlers and older children.

If you receive a phone call asking if children are invited, that will be your opportunity to clarify that only adults will be attending the ceremony and to state whether children are invited to the reception. Once you make your decision, there should be no exceptions. It is sure to alienate guests when they realize that other children were invited while their children were not.

Be aware that, if there are a few younger children in the wedding party, some guests automatically assume that children are invited. And then there are those few who bring along their children even when they have been asked not to do so.

Invitation Wording for Encore Weddings

It used to be there wasn't much variation in the wording of wedding invitations. Since the bride's mom and dad were footing the bill, they were the ones to "request your presence at the wedding of. . . ." But now, divorce and remarriage have affected even the wording of the wedding invitation, so changes must be made. Wedding invitations for encore weddings can be anything from traditional to quite creative. The wording is up to you, especially if both partners were previously married. This is where many get confused. I am often asked, "Because of divorce and remarriage, there are now so many people in my extended family. Must I name each one on the invitation?" Following are some examples of encore wedding invitations for just about every situation.

When the bride and groom issue their own invitations:

The honour of your presence
is requested
at the marriage of
Rebecca Jean Connelly
to
Steven Charles Bradley
on
Saturday, the fourth of June
Two thousand and seven
at four o'clock in the afternoon
Christian Country Church
Santa Barbara, California

When a couple would like to include the names of their children:

Rebecca Jean Connelly and Steven Charles Bradley
together with their children
Samantha Alexander and Susan Bradley
request the honour of your presence
at their marriage
on the fourth of June
Two thousand and seven
at four o'clock

Christian Country Church
Santa Barbara, California

If the bride is a widow or divorced:

The honour of your presence
is requested at the marriage of
Mrs. Rebecca Jean Connelly
to
Mr. Steven Charles Bradley
Saturday, the fourth of June
Two thousand and seven
at four o'clock
Christian Country Church
Santa Barbara, California

If the divorced or widowed bride feels the title *Mrs.* is too formal, she may choose not to use it.

When the bride and groom's adult children are hosting the wedding, then their names may appear on the invitation. The bride's children (with their spouses if they are married) are listed first, then the groom's children. They are listed oldest to youngest.

Mrs. Mary Lions
Mr. and Mrs. Larry Ford
Mr. and Mrs. Mark Bradley
Mr. Scott Bradley
request the honour of your presence
at the marriage of their parents
Rebecca Jean Connelly
to
Steven Charles Bradley

In the example above, the older daughter of Rebecca Jean Connelly is divorced and uses her married last name. The next one listed
is Rebecca Jean's younger daughter, who is married to Larry Ford.
They could have also been listed as "Bridget and Larry Ford." The
bride or groom's child is always listed before his or her spouse if both
first names are used. The next couple listed, Mr. and Mrs. Mark
Bradley, are Steven Bradley's older son and his wife. They could also
have been listed as "Mark and Louise Bradley." If Louise and Mark
were not married but considered themselves life partners, they could
be listed as "Mr. Mark Bradley and Ms. Louise Lewis." Mr. Scott
Bradley is Steven Bradley's younger son. Courtesy titles can be left off
if the people hosting the wedding prefer a less formal tone.

When guests are invited to a reception that immediately follows
the ceremony, then this should be noted at the bottom of the invitation:

Reception immediately following at
Discovery Bay Country Club
Discovery Bay, California

It is not uncommon for a second wedding to be small and private
but have a large reception. The reception can follow the wedding or be
held at another time. If this is your preference, you may want to invite
the guests to the wedding personally (face-to-face or by phone) and then
send an invitation to the reception that looks similar to this one:

Rebecca Jean and Steven Charles Bradley
request the pleasure of your company
at the reception of their marriage
Saturday, the fourth of June
Two thousand and seven
at four o'clock
Discovery Bay Country Club
Discovery Bay, California

All of the above encore invitations include somewhat formal wording. If your wedding will be more casual, you may want a warmer feel to the invitation. In that case, you may want to try:

Our joy will be more complete if you share in the marriage of . . .

[names] request the pleasure of your company at the marriage of . . .

With joyful hearts we ask you to be present at the ceremony uniting [names] in marriage.

Please join us as we celebrate the marriage of . . .

If it is a holiday wedding, you may want to say:

In the spirit of peace and joy [or of the season] *the parents of [name] request the honor of your presence* . . .

Additional suggestions for wording will probably be available where you order your invitations. Remember, the wording of your wedding invitation, like your vows, is really up to you. If you feel most comfortable using standardized wording, then use it, but it is also perfectly acceptable to use your own.

The Guest List and Invitations for Adult Children of Divorce

When those with divorced parents get married, the guest list begins with the bride and groom's parents. It then proceeds through the other family members and then to friends. It can get quite complicated if both sets of parents are divorced. You may then have to coordinate four different guest lists—the bride's parents have two separate lists (one for Mom and one for Dad), and so do the groom's parents.

Guest List Out of Control

"The size of our wedding has become far larger than I ever wanted or than my parents can afford. My fiancé's parents are divorced. We said his side of the family could invite fifty guests. My soon-to-be mother-in-law invited fifty guests, none of whom are from my fiancé's father's side of the family. Now he wants to invite fifty more guests. Everyone is so upset. My fiancé and I just want to elope."

Many times when things of this sort happen, it is because the divorced parents of the adult child getting married are so used to trying to outdo each other that they don't realize that the one they are hurting with their bad behavior is not the ex, but their beloved child. If someone sat down with your mother-in-law and said, "Do you realize that you are frustrating your child so much that he wants to elope?" it is doubtful that she would respond, "You know, I don't even care. My ex is such a jerk, he deserves all this."

The rules of good ex-etiquette remind divorced parents that it is time to worry about something bigger than themselves. The rules also teach children of divorce that it is time to stand up for themselves and make their parents accountable.

In this case, your future mother-in-law invited too many people, and so she is the one who is responsible for making amends. She can either call the extra friends and relatives, apologize for the misunderstanding, and rescind the invitations, or she can expect to pay for their dinners, plus the extra alcohol and drinks, place settings, waiters and waitresses, etc.

The easiest way to prevent something like this from happening is to split the amount of allotted invitations in half before telling the divorced parents the number of people they can invite. So, if the bride's guest list is limited to fifty people, tell Mom she can invite twenty-five people and Dad he can invite twenty-five people.

Inviting an Absentee Parent

> *"My father has never been there for me, except when it's convenient for him. I know he loves me, but I can't tell you how many times I waited by the door and he never showed up. I know I hold a grudge. I'm thinking I shouldn't even invite my dad to my wedding at all."*

If you do not invite your dad because it will make you feel more comfortable on your special day, that's one thing, and completely your prerogative. If you are doing it to get back at him for being a bad father all these years, then that's being spiteful, and in the end it may not make you feel as good as you think it will. Only you can make that call.

If you have decided that you do not want to invite him, remember good ex-etiquette rule number eight, "Be honest and straightforward." That means if you choose not to invite your dad, before the invitations go out, tell him why. It will only complicate issues if he hears that you are getting married through the grapevine. Then you are acting no better than he has all these years. The ultimate goal of using good ex-etiquette is to *stop* the bad behavior, not perpetuate it.

How do you tell him of your decision? If it's too difficult to talk to him, write him a letter or an e-mail. Be gentle but direct, simply explaining how you feel. Let him know that the door is open for an improved relationship in the future by suggesting a face-to-face talk, or even offering to attend counseling with him when you return from your honeymoon.

Inviting "the Other Woman (or Man)"

> *"I am getting married in two months. My parents are divorced, and my father has been dating a woman, Valerie, for four months. My siblings and I have all met her, but our mom has*

not. Should I invite her to the wedding, or would that be a slap in the face to my mom?"

The fact that your mom hasn't met your dad's new girlfriend is not the reason she should or should not be invited. Those marrying decide upon the guest list (as I've said many times, it's your wedding, not your parents'), so if you desire Valerie's presence as your dad's guest, then she should be invited.

That said, there is a particular situation in which the child marrying should take his or her parent's desires into consideration. If there was an affair, and Dad or Mom is openly dating the person with whom he or she had the affair, then it would probably be hurtful for them to appear together when the divorce is still fresh.

But if there was no recent affair that prompted your parents' separation, and Valerie appears to be a permanent fixture, inviting her is appropriate—but try not to let your wedding be the first time she and your mom meet. Valerie will likely be attending other family get-togethers, so encourage them to use the time before the wedding to meet and lay the groundwork for cordial interaction. Hopefully, your mom will do this, not because she necessarily wants to be pals with her ex's new partner, but for your sake.

On the other hand, if Dad's girlfriend is just that, a female who is a friend, it may not be necessary to invite her at this time. You can make that decision.

"My dad left my mom after thirty years of marriage for a new woman. They've been together about four years now, even though my parents still haven't divorced, and I'm still uncomfortable with her. We get along OK, but I felt pressured into inviting her to my wedding against my better judgment. A few days after the invitation arrived, I called her and explained that, though I want us to be friendly, I would rather she not

attend my wedding, for the sake of my mom. I feel a little guilty now; was this using really bad manners?"

In general, it is very poor ex-etiquette to uninvite a guest. But in this case, actually, I don't think your manners were really that bad. You were honest and straightforward, you said that you did not openly harbor bad will, and you expressed a desire to have a relationship in the future. Those are all examples of good ex-etiquette. In my opinion, your response was quite magnanimous, considering your dad openly left your mother for a relationship with this woman and is legally still married to your mother.

The one thing you did incorrectly was adding her name (or "and guest") to your dad's invitation in the first place. Ideally, you would have discussed your concerns with his girlfriend exactly the way you did, but *before* the invitations went out, and then just listed only your father on the invitation.

"My mother has been living with Mike, her fiancé, for two years. She has been separated from my father for several years, but they are still not officially divorced. I am getting married in a couple of months, and I worry that my father will be embarrassed in public if my mother shows up with Mike, even though Mike was not the reason behind my parents' separation. To complicate things, my sister doesn't really accept Mike and is, at times, openly rude to him. I recently told my mom that because of all the drama, I have decided not to invite Mike to the wedding. She says that he is hurt by my decision. That was not my intention. Was this poor ex-etiquette?"

It is still regarded as very poor manners to attend a family gathering with a man or woman who is not yet divorced when his or her ex is present. If your mother insists that Mike be invited (although it's rather tacky of her to do so), here's what you could do. First, check with your father to see if he would be offended by Mike's presence. If he would not, and you then feel comfortable inviting him, do so. However, if your father does express discomfort with the new partner attending, it's best to honor his request and ask Mom not to bring Mike to the wedding. Remember, this is based on the fact that the original parties are not yet divorced. Once they are divorced, the ex need not be consulted.

Your other concern appears to be the drama—the behind-the-scenes gossip, your sister's rudeness, and how all that will affect your wedding day. And it is your right to make the judgment call as you see fit. However, when you do that, you run the risk of hurt feelings. That doesn't mean you used bad ex-etiquette. It means you took a stand. In regard to your sister's attitude toward Mike, your family members' acceptance of a new partner is largely determined by how the new partner is presented. If your mother wants Mike to be accepted, she must make her regard and respect for him obvious. Family members will usually follow her lead.

Here's a suggestion for how Mom can communicate respect for her new partner, put your sister on notice, and publicly display respect for your father. Perhaps a couple of weeks before the wedding, at a family dinner hosted by your mother and her new partner, Mom can propose a toast that makes her feelings obvious. She can say something like:

> *Now, let's lift our glasses to my daughter's excellent choice, Steven.* [The mother turns to Steven.] *Mike and I are so happy to have you as a member of our family. And I have also spoken to Rebecca's* [the daughter's] *father, and I know that he is pleased, too. We all look forward to a lovely wedding and wish you an equally lovely life together. To Rebecca and Steven!*

That should make where things stand apparent to everyone—including your sister. In that short toast your mother has let everyone attending know that the relationship between her new partner and her ex is amicable, and that she welcomes your fiancé. If your sister is listening, she will realize that she is alone in her refusal to accept Mike, and it's just a waste of time to keep the family in turmoil.

But remember, this is a toast to be given at a private dinner hosted by your mother and Mike, *not* at the rehearsal dinner or at the reception, in front of your father. Openly flaunting a new relationship while the ex is present is not good ex-etiquette, even if the ex openly acknowledges the new relationship, as it appears your father does.

Inviting an Ex-Bonusparent

"I am getting married this fall. My mother was married to my stepdad for ten years and divorced last year. He has been in my life since I was a young girl, and I want to invite him to my wedding. My mom is fuming. Because she hates him, I can't invite him to my wedding? One other thing, their three-year-old daughter, my half-sister, will be my flower girl. It doesn't seem fair that her daddy can't see her all dressed up."

Many divorced people feel as your mother does. They expect their relatives' allegiance after their divorce, thinking to themselves, "If I don't get along with him, you can't either" or "If you really loved me, you wouldn't side with that jerk." The truth is, it has nothing to do with siding with anyone; rather, you've formed a relationship with your mother's ex over the years that's completely separate from your relationship with her, and that relationship means something to you. You also recognize that your mom's ex-husband is also the father of your half-sister, and you understand the need to continue to interact positively for the sake of the little girl.

Bottom line, in this day and age, when the divorce rate is 50 percent, if people started eliminating everyone who is someone's ex from the invitation list, very few people would be invited. That's why it's best that you have a heart-to-heart with your mother, explain your point of view, invite everyone whom you want to invite, and let each person decide if he or she wants to attend.

Some may question this reasoning; after all, she's your mother. And there are always extenuating circumstances that may lead to another conclusion (for instance, if a stepparent was violent or abusive, it would be inappropriate to invite him or her). But in general, this is what I suggest. Out of respect for the bride and groom and the importance of the day, everyone who attends should act like adults. I suggest you all go light on the alcohol, though. Alcohol can loosen the inhibitions and the tongue. Kids will be watching, and if you think there is even a chance of a scene, help Mom stay away from the booze. Another helpful hint: delegate a close friend to keep an eye on the ex-couple; if she anticipates there might be words, she should quickly get your ex-stepdad out on the dance floor.

Invitation Wording for Adult Children of Divorce

The following examples are designed to help you understand how to list the family members on wedding invitations when the parents of the bride or groom are divorced and/or remarried. A traditional invitation, issued by the bride's parents, is presented first as a reference point:

Mr. and Mrs. Douglas Morrison
request the honour of your presence
at the marriage of their daughter
Sara Anne
to
Kenneth Michael Miller
Saturday, the twentieth of June
Two thousand and seven
at four o'clock
Christian Country Church
Santa Barbara, California

When the parents of the bride are divorced, their names are not written on the same line:

Mrs. Louise Smith Johnson
and
Mr. Douglas Morrison
request the honour of your presence
at the marriage of their daughter
Sara Anne
to
Kenneth Michael Miller
Saturday, the twentieth of June
Two thousand and seven
at four o'clock
Christian Country Church
Santa Barbara, California

In the above example, the mother's maiden name is Smith. Depending on what name she now chooses to go by, she could be listed as any of the following:

Louise Smith
Ms. Louise Smith
Mrs. Louise Johnson
Ms. Louise Johnson
Louise Smith Johnson

When the mother is divorced and has not remarried, but issues the invitations alone:

Mrs. Louise Smith Johnson
requests the honour of your presence

at the marriage of her daughter
Sara Anne
to
Kenneth Michael Miller
Saturday, the twentieth of June
Two thousand and seven
at four o'clock
Christian Country Church
Santa Barbara, California

Again, the mother could go by any of the alternatives listed above. When the mother has remarried and issues the invitations with the father:

Mrs. Braden Stephenson
and
Mr. Douglas Morrison
request the honour of your presence
at the marriage of their daughter
Sara Anne Morrison
to
Kenneth Michael Miller
Saturday, the twentieth of June
Two thousand and seven
at four o'clock
Christian Country Church
Santa Barbara, California

Note that the daughter's last name is listed in this invitation because the mother's and the daughter's last names are no longer the same now that the mother has remarried and taken her new husband's name. Mrs. Braden Stephenson may also be listed as:

Mrs. Louise Smith Stephenson
Louise Stephenson
Ms. Louise Stephenson

When the bride's mother has remarried and issues the ceremony invitation alone, without the bonusfather:

Mrs. Braden Stephenson
requests the honour of your presence
at the marriage of her daughter
Sara Anne Morrison
to
Kenneth Michael Miller
Saturday, the twentieth of June
Two thousand and seven
at four o'clock
Christian Country Church
Santa Barbara, California

When the mother is remarried and issues the invitations with the bonusfather:

Mr. and Mrs. Braden Stephenson
request the honour of your presence
at the marriage of her daughter
Sara Anne Morrison
to
Kenneth Michael Miller
Saturday, the twentieth of June
Two thousand and seven
at four o'clock
Christian Country Church
Santa Barbara, California

When describing the daughter, Sara Anne Morrison, in a joint invitation from mother and bonusfather, there are three alternatives:

her daughter [as in the above example]
Mrs. Stephenson's daughter
their daughter

"Their daughter" is used when the biological father is deceased, out of the picture, or on such friendly terms with the mother and bonusfather that he has agreed his daughter can be listed as "their daughter." When there is a question of offending the biological parent, this phrase should not be used.

When the bride's mother has remarried and the father has not remarried, but the invitation is issued jointly:

Mr. and Mrs. Braden Stephenson
and
Mr. Douglas Morrison
request the honour of your presence
at the marriage of their daughter
Sara Anne Morrison
to
Kenneth Michael Miller
Saturday, the twentieth of June
Two thousand and seven
at four o'clock
Christian Country Church
Santa Barbara, California

When a parent is living with a partner but is not married, it may or may not be appropriate to list the partner on the invitation. If the two have been regarded as a long-time couple by family members, then you may list them as follows:

Mr. and Mrs. Braden Stephenson
and
Mr. Douglas Morrison and Ms. Brenda Wilson
request the honour of your presence
at the marriage of their daughter
Sara Anne Morrison
to
Kenneth Michael Miller
Saturday, the twentieth of June
Two thousand and seven
at four o'clock
Christian Country Church
Santa Barbara, California

When the bride's father is not remarried and issues the invitation alone:

Mr. Douglas Morrison
requests the honour of your presence
at the marriage of his daughter
Sara Anne
to
Kenneth Michael Miller
Saturday, the twentieth of June
Two thousand and seven
at four o'clock
Christian Country Church
Santa Barbara, California

When the bride's father has remarried and issues the invitation with the bonusmother:

Mr. and Mrs. Douglas Morrison
request the honour of your presence
at the marriage of his daughter
Sara Anne
to
Kenneth Michael Miller
Saturday, the twentieth of June
Two thousand and seven
at four o'clock
Christian Country Church
Santa Barbara, California

When describing Sara Anne Morrison, there are again three alternatives:

his daughter [as in the above example]
Mr. Morrison's daughter
their daughter

Again, if there is a possibility that the other parent will take offense, the phrase "their daughter" should not be used.

When the father has remarried and the mother is not married, but the invitation is issued jointly:

Mrs. Louise Smith Morrison [or just Morrison]
and
Mr. and Mrs. Douglas Morrison
request the honour of your presence
at the marriage of their daughter
Sara Anne
to

Kenneth Michael Miller
Saturday, the twentieth of June
Two thousand and seven
at four o'clock
Christian Country Church
Santa Barbara, California

If the mother is not contributing to the wedding but is still listed on the invitation, then the father and bonusmother's names should appear first:

Mr. and Mrs. Douglas Morrison
and
Mrs. Louise Smith Morrison [or just Morrison]
request the honour of your presence
at the marriage of their daughter
Sara Anne
to
Kenneth Michael Miller
Saturday, the twentieth of June
Two thousand and seven
at four o'clock
Christian Country Church
Santa Barbara, California

When the mother and father have both remarried and issue invitations together without new spouses:

Mrs. Braden Stephenson
and
Mr. Douglas Morrison
request the honour of your presence
at the marriage of their daughter

Sara Anne Morrison

to

Kenneth Michael Miller

Saturday, the twentieth of June

Two thousand and seven

at four o'clock

Christian Country Church

Santa Barbara, California

In the case below, the parents are divorced and both mother and father are remarried. The daughter is not that close with the stepmother. But because her stepmother is married to her father, and he is helping to give the wedding, the stepmom is regarded as a hostess of the affair. Therefore, she should be listed on the invitations with the father. The mother of the bride and her new spouse are listed first, and then the father of the bride and his new spouse. All of them jointly invite the guests to the wedding of their daughter. (If referring to the bride as "their daughter" is offensive to anyone—though it's petty, technically she is the bonusdaughter, not the daughter, of two of them—then simply using her name will suffice.)

Mr. and Mrs. Braden Stephenson

and

Mr. and Mrs. Douglas Morrison

request the honour of your presence

at the marriage of their daughter

Sara Anne Morrison

to

Kenneth Michael Miller

Saturday, the twentieth of June

Two thousand and seven

at four o'clock

Christian Country Church

Santa Barbara, California

If the parents of the groom have helped to host the wedding and wish to be added to the invitation:

Mr. and Mrs. Braden Stephenson
Mr. and Mrs. Douglas Morrison
Mr. and Mrs. James Miller
request the honour of your presence
at the marriage of
Sara Anne Morrison
to
Kenneth Michael Miller
Saturday, the twentieth of June
Two thousand and seven
at four o'clock
Christian Country Church
Santa Barbara, California

To avoid confusion when there may be quite a few names to list on the invitation, such as when both the bride and the groom's parents have been divorced and are remarried, a good alternative is:

Together with their families
Sara Anne Morrison
and
Kenneth Michael Miller
Request the honour of your presence . . .

Alternately, "Together with their families" may be listed after the names of the bride and groom.

7

Showers and Bachelor and Bachelorette Parties

L egend has it that the first bridal shower was given for a Dutch
bride who chose to marry a man with very little money. The
bride's father disliked his daughter's choice and would not
give her a dowry. The couple married in spite of the father's
objections, but still needed the necessities, so the community chipped
in to help. The couple was "showered" with gifts, and since that day,
when a couple marries they are often given gifts from family and
friends in order to help them start their life together. Showers provide
the mainstay of a first-time bride's household items, from blenders to

toasters to coffeemakers. A bridal shower makes it easy to set up housekeeping.

Bridal showers are also perfectly acceptable for encore brides, but many have been out on their own for years and do not need the same sort of gifts offered to the first-time bride. Some may still look to the shower for necessities, but most see their encore bridal shower as a way to celebrate their transition from single to married life, by receiving little luxuries they would not normally buy for themselves or taking one last vacation with the girls. If this is the case, a theme shower may be the most appropriate. A theme shower centers around a specific category of gift, like books or linens or even wine. I have been to a shower that specified "bathroom accessories." The bride was redoing all the bathrooms and was ecstatic about the theme.

Ex-Etiquette for Showers

Who Hosts the Bridal Shower?

The maid of honor, who is usually the bride-to-be's closest friend, or all the bridesmaids and other good friends are most often the ones to host a bridal shower. Parents and sisters, either biological or bonus, and other extended family members may help, and even offer their homes as the site for the shower, but they shouldn't officially host it. This is because bridal showers are supposed to show the support of the community for the marriage, and it would appear self-serving for a relative to host a celebration with the sole purpose of acquiring presents for a family member.

> *"My mother is marrying for the third time—both of her previous husbands, including my dad, have passed away. May I give her a bridal shower?"*

If you are asking whether it is correct for an older woman to have a shower, the answer is yes, of course. But, technically, a daughter shouldn't give her mother a shower. You can offer to have a get-together at your home and cosponsor it with her close friends.

Whom to Invite

Usually, only women attend bridal showers. The bride prepares the guest list and passes it on to the person hosting the shower. No one should ever be invited to a bridal shower who is not invited to the wedding.

The invitation list starts with the bride and groom's mothers and grandmothers, aunts, cousins, and good friends, as well as older daughters of both partners. Bonusmoms should also be included on the guest list if relations between the biological mother and the bonus-mother are cordial.

> *"I'm having a shower, and I'm really sweating the guest list. My mom and bonusmom cannot be in the same room together. If I don't invite my bonusmom to my wedding shower, I know she will be hurt—but my mother will be fuming if she is there."*

If you as the bride are faced with this question, you have two choices. You can invite them both, explain up front that this is the way it is, and suggest they work it out before they come to your shower and embarrass you in public. Or you can have two showers—one for one side of the family and one for the other—and invite half your friends to one, half your friends to the other. But the hostess and bride should not stress about the guest list. The hostess is generously volunteering her time, money, and energy to organize a shower for her friend, the bride. The guests invited to the shower are there to help the bride celebrate her good fortune. And guests are always expected to be gracious when entering someone's home or the establishment chosen to accommodate the affair.

> *"My former husband was killed in an accident. Although his parents have passed, I have remained quite close with his sister and his aunt. Both know I am remarrying and are very happy for me. Should they be invited to my bridal shower?"*

Since the bride prepares the guest list, anyone she feels it is important to include should be invited to the bridal shower. Under the circumstances it is understandable if she has stayed close to these former relatives. It is important to remember, however, that if they are invited to the shower, they must also be invited to the wedding, and this could open another can of worms. New relatives should not be put in the position of being surprised by ex-relatives during an introduction. Special care should be taken to introduce past and present relatives before the shower or wedding takes place.

> *"I've lived with my fiancé for seven years, and over those years I have become quite good friends with his children's mother. Should she be invited to my bridal shower?"*

No matter how close a past and present partner become over the years, it is inappropriate for the past partner to attend the present partner's bridal shower. A past partner's presence may spark some inappropriate comparisons that could embarrass both women and, more important, any children who may be present.

Even so, there may be times when this rule can be overlooked. For example, a person sometimes stays friendly with someone he dated in high school or college, and then the old friend becomes friendly with his fiancée. If this is the case, and the bride-to-be is comfortable with the friend attending the shower, it is acceptable to add her name to the guest list.

If you are a former partner and you find yourself in this situation, out of respect for the bride-to-be, be careful how you present your friendship to others attending the event. If asked how you know the bride-to-be, the kindest response would be something like, "I have been friends with Michael since high school." Not "Michael was my first love, and we have remained friends over the years. Now I am friends with Lisa." That implies intimacy with Michael, and although Lisa may be over it, having her friends and acquaintances know about it may still embarrass her. With that in mind, if you are now truly friends with Lisa, your allegiance should lie with her. In order to prevent gossip, it is your duty to present the relationship appropriately.

"I'm getting remarried and have many of the same friends now as I did the first time around. I recently heard that it was improper for people to attend both the first and the second bridal showers. But I want my friends there!"

In the past, proper etiquette did suggest that the same people should not attend the encore shower as attended the shower for the first wedding. This is no longer the rule. A friend who has attended a first bridal shower may certainly attend another. Though it's not mandatory for those attending the second shower to bring a gift, I think it's a good idea to do so, even if it's something small, like a bottle of wine, a candle, or pink fuzzy slippers.

"I have thirteen-year-old twin daughters and a bonusdaughter-to-be who is eleven. I would love to include all of them on the guest list for my bridal shower. Are they too young to attend?"

A bride-to-be often looks for ways to include her children from a previous marriage or other young relatives in the wedding preparations, and a bridal shower may be the perfect answer. It's a great way to allow older children and teens to be involved right from the start. They can help pick out a theme, assist with the planning and color choices, make favors, greet and seat the guests, and keep records for thank you notes. It will help them to feel included, and that will aid the bonding process among all the new bonusfamily members.

Shower Gifts

One of my favorite gifts from my encore bridal shower was from a dear friend from high school who had seen me at both my best and my worst. She gave me a book of love poems by Emily Dickinson and a great bottle of wine with two wine glasses. She also gave me a Mickey Mouse nightshirt and fuzzy slippers, which got huge laughs at the shower. She had stolen mine at a slumber party twenty years before; the gift celebrated our very long friendship. Hers are the only presents I still remember to this day. So, you see, a meaningful present need not be expensive or "appropriate." Most etiquette books would not say that fuzzy slippers are the correct gift to present at a bridal shower. I am of a different mind. I think presents should be offered and accepted with earnest best wishes for the future, and those are the only criteria necessary.

> "My new husband's family includes his ex-wife in every family event. There was a family wedding shower recently, and I was not invited, but my husband's ex-wife was. I would like to send a gift anyway, because I like my husband's nephew and his fiancée. Is it appropriate to send a gift?"

Of course, your husband's family could be acting rude on purpose, but more often than not in these situations, the family have established a longtime relationship with the ex, love her, and still want to include her in the family functions. If they do that, they probably feel as if they can't include you, so they don't. That's the reason, but it's not a good excuse for poor ex-etiquette.

The only connection this family has with your husband's ex is their affection for her, and that puts everyone in a very sticky situation. I will not suggest that the family shun the ex-wife, but I will suggest that your husband have a heart-to-heart talk with his relatives and explain that as his wife, you should be the one to participate in family functions. Good ex-etiquette states that the family may have to learn to carry on their relationship with his ex at times other than family get-togethers.

As for the upcoming wedding shower, always stay as pleasant as you can, and do send a present with a card expressing your heartfelt wish for the couple's happiness. When they receive it, it will tastefully alert them to their poor ex-etiquette.

Shower Games

> *"How do I keep things moving along? I'm afraid everyone will be terribly bored. And I'm a little nervous about having past and present relatives all in the same room. Help!"*

First of all, few rank bridal or baby showers at the top of their entertainment list. Everyone who attends a shower knows why she is there—to offer the bride a gift to help her on her way. So from that point of view, it's really nothing to worry about. That said, showers can be quite boring unless the hostess gets creative, assigns a theme, and thinks things through before the guests arrive. That's the reason games are often played before the bride opens her gifts. It's a way to pass the time and offer a nice little prize to one or two of the guests for winning the game. Games are also a great way to break the ice between guests who would normally not interact with each other—mom and bonusmom or past and future sisters-in-law, for example. Games get their minds off of each other and onto positive interaction. If you have guests of this sort—past and future relatives who may have a problem interacting—do not pick team games that place one on one team and one on the other. Although you may think they will act like adults, competition of any sort will just reinforce tension between them.

Some encore brides may find shower games downright silly and opt for a high tea or a night with friends at a favorite getaway.

How Many Showers?

"I have never been married, but my fiancé has been. I want the whole thing—the showers, the big wedding—and my friends are so excited that I am getting married that they all want to give me a shower. How many showers can I have without seeming tacky?"

In general, I'd say two. Many people have one women-only shower hosted by the maid of honor and one couples shower.

However, there are times when even more showers are acceptable. For example, if the bride's parents are divorced, and the bride has developed a close relationship with her bonusmother, but the bonus-mother and the mother of the bride cannot find a way to get along, then separate showers may be given: one for the bride's friends, one for the mother's side of the family, and one for the father's side of the family. When handled this way, most would attend only one shower and possibly the couples shower as well. However, a sticky question still remains with this scenario: Which shower would the groom's side of the family attend? The shower given for the bride's mother's side of the family or the one for the bride's father's side of the family? Because of the mom and bonusmom's inability to get along, new family members are asked to choose sides right from the beginning. This is a perfect example of why it is essential for divorced parents and their new partners to put their issues aside for the sake of their children. If they don't, family feuds are passed from generation to generation, gaining momentum as family members are added and expected to take sides.

Bridal Registry

"When I was married the first time, my parents paid for a huge wedding, and I registered for shower and wedding gifts at some of the finest stores. My marriage ended in divorce after five years. Is it appropriate to register again now that I am marrying for the second time?"

Although many people think a shower registry is for first-time brides only, it's appropriate to register every time you marry. Since encore brides and grooms are often already set up in life, friends and family may be at a loss as to what to get them for a shower or wedding gift. Registering will make it much easier for your guests to pick out exactly what you want—and need. Many encore couples register at less traditional stores. For example, if you and your intended are avid readers or music lovers, register with Barnes and Noble or Amazon.com. If you like to work in the garden, try stores like Home Depot or Target. For other special gift ideas, see the "Resources" section at the back of this book.

Combining a Baby Shower and a Bridal Shower

"I'm pregnant, and my shower hostess was wondering if she could combine my bridal and baby showers. Is that ever done?"

If it is common knowledge that you are pregnant, then it is perfectly fine to combine both showers. If you have not let the outside world know that you are pregnant, then obviously you will want to keep the news to yourself until you are ready to make that announcement, and just have a bridal shower.

Here's a wonderful idea volunteered by a Bonus Families member: "When my seven-year-old bonusson was receiving two new baby siblings, one from each side, within three months of each other, my husband and I decided to throw him a 'big brother party.' We had it on the same day as our baby/adult couples shower. We hired a babysitter to oversee the party, let my bonusson invite a few of his friends, and told them the theme of the party was celebrating being a big brother. The kids came to our adult shower temporarily to share the presents they received. It was a little break for us, and a couple of the guys told quick little stories about how cool it was to be a big brother. By the time the shower was over, my bonusson thought being a big brother was about the greatest thing there was."

Bachelor and Bachelorette Parties

In more traditional times, brides had bridesmaids' teas or luncheons, and grooms had bachelor dinners, as a way to thank their chosen attendants for their support and spend some time with them before the ceremony. Today, a bachelor or bachelorette party is viewed more as a rite of passage marking the bride or groom's shift from single to married life, and it often include strippers and other lewd and lascivious behavior. Over the years these parties have gotten more and more outrageous and have been at the root of many a wedding postponement. The bottom line is that there is very little etiquette assigned to bachelor and bachelorette parties, and I will not attempt to apply etiquette to them now.

Even though bachelor and bachelorette parties are usually given for first-time brides and grooms, it may be something the encore bride or groom did not experience the first time and feels compelled to have this time around. Or if years and years have passed between marriages, the bride and groom may have a new life and new friends, and a bachelor or bachelorette party may just seem fitting. This is perfectly acceptable, and a great way to let off steam before the big day. Encore bachelor and bachelorette parties are typically a little less raucous. An older bachelor might opt for a poker night with his buddies, while the older encore bride might prefer something more subdued than all-night drinking in Vegas. Below are some great ideas for calmer, more conservative bachelor and bachelorette parties for the encore bride or groom:

- Day or weekend of golf with close friends
- Football or baseball game with box seats. If your favorite team is playing out of town, take a road trip with friends to watch them play.
- Poker night with pals. Rent a room at a great hotel, hire a bartender, and cater your favorite foods. Or have it at a friend's home, but hire someone to serve and clean up!
- A NASCAR or Supercross getaway weekend
- Weekend of camping, fishing, or scuba diving
- Spa day with massages, facials, pedicures, and manicures
- Weekend of lounging at the beach
- Ski weekend for winter weddings
- Night of dancing out on the town
- Weekend or dinner cruise

Whom to Invite

"Is it appropriate to invite my dad and my bonusdad to my bachelor party?"

It's not uncommon for the father of the groom to attend a getaway weekend with the groom and his buddies. His attendance is questionable if the bachelor party is going to be a crazy, raucous affair, however. You don't want to embarrass him.

If the groom's bonusdad and father get along, it is perfectly permissible that they both attend the groom's bachelor party. A bachelor party is not a time to start mending fences, however. Look to lay the groundwork for positive interaction between Dad and Bonusdad well before the plans for the bachelor party are in place. This holds true for Mom and Bonusmom as well. It's fine to invite them both to a bachelorette party, but make sure their relationship is cordial. If you invite people to spend time together who have a history of not getting along, and you add even a little alcohol, you have the makings of a mess. Make sure they have made their peace before the invitations go out.

"*My fiancé is still friends with his ex, who was his high-school sweetheart. She's a longtime friend of his family, but she's still his ex. He is also best friends with her brother. She's not in our wedding, but my fiancé wants me to invite her to my bachelorette party because he is inviting her brother. Granted, it's been ten years, but it still makes me uncomfortable. What do I do?*"

You may not care if you ever see her again, but if this woman is a friend of your fiancé's family, and his best friend's sister, you must address the problem. Honesty is the best policy in cases like this. If you are uncomfortable with her attending the party, the best thing to do is just tell her—as tactfully as possible. Don't depend on your fiancé or her brother to tell her. You are an adult, and it's your problem. Understand, however, that if you take this tack, it will most likely impact your future communication. If you have been hiding your uneasiness, admitting it now will bring it to the forefront and may stifle any relationship you already have—but that may be exactly what is needed. It could give you both the opportunity to air your differences, and the discussion may pave the way for a more comfortable invitation. At any rate, don't put it off or openly shun her. Since she is a family friend, you will insult more people than just her if you take that approach. Take care of it in an honest and open way, and you will always come out on top.

Bachelor Party Necessary for Encore Groom?

"My fiancée has never been married, but I have. She wants to have a bachelorette party, but I feel a little uncomfortable having a bachelor party because I already had one ten years ago, when I was married the first time. My fiancée says if she's having one, I have to have one. Is that true?"

Just because one person would like to have a bachelor or bachelorette party, the other is not obliged to follow suit, especially in this case, when you already had a party before your previous marriage. Many people stay close with old friends for years and years, and it could be that the people you would invite to a second bachelor party already attended the first one. In that case, it would not be appropriate to have another conventional bachelor party. It would, however, be appropriate to have a less raucous get-together with friends, if you like, before you marry for the second time.

8
The Rehearsal Dinner

R ehearsal dinners have not always been part of the wedding festivities, but they have evolved into an important aspect of wedding preparation. A wonderful meal is a great way to set the tone for the next day's festivities, to thank your parents and attendants for their support, to welcome out-of-town guests, and to allow any guests who may be meeting for the first time an opportunity to get to know each other. Plus, the rehearsal dinner is the last time the wedding party can review the schedule for the ceremony and reception before the big day. Remember, even if the bride and groom opt for a formal wedding, the rehearsal dinner need not be formal. For smaller, more casual weddings, for which a wedding rehearsal is not required, some couples may still want to host a nice dinner before the ceremony.

Your rehearsal dinner guest list should include most everyone who was at the wedding rehearsal. The dinner is held immediately following the rehearsal and includes the wedding party, parents and bonusparents of the bride and groom, grandparents of the bride and groom, the officiant and his or her spouse, the parents of the flower girl and ring bearer (probably not the flower girl and ring bearer themselves, however, because they are usually very young), and the soloist, if one is performing during the service. Out-of-town guests who arrive before the wedding are often invited too, but if many guests attend from out of town, and you have to cut the guest list somewhere, they are the most obvious choice.

Considerations for Encore Couples

Since they've done all this before, some encore couples may not feel the need to have a rehearsal dinner; it might just seem like one more expense. But instead of putting the kibosh on the night altogether, encore couples could look at the rehearsal dinner as a time to celebrate new combined-family unity. If there are children from a previous marriage, the rehearsal dinner is an ideal time to include them in the wedding festivities. Great ways to make kids feel special and involved at rehearsal dinners are giving them places of honor at the table and making special toasts welcoming them into the family. Toasts can be made by not only new bonusparents, but also extended family members like aunts, uncles, and cousins. If the bride or groom has divorced parents with new partners in attendance, those parents and bonusparents can make mutual toasts pledging to support the new couple and to co-grandparent their grandchildren and bonus-grandchildren with love and respect.

Considerations for Those with Divorced Parents

"My mother has been best friends with my fiancé's mother for years. My fiancé's mother and father were recently divorced,

and his dad immediately remarried someone quite a bit younger. My mother is furious and does not want my fiancé's stepmother to attend any of my wedding festivities—especially the rehearsal dinner, which will be small and, hopefully, quiet. But my father-in-law will be paying for the dinner! What do I do?"

Although your mother's allegiance to her friend is admirable, it's not her wedding, and her behavior is putting you in a very awkward position. The invitations to the rehearsal dinner are dictated by who is in the wedding party, and if you look at it like that, no one really has control over who is invited. As the wife of the father of the groom, it is standard that she be included. The only people you can really opt to not include at this point are out-of-town guests.

Truthfully, your mother needs to realize what she is doing by demanding that you not invite your fiancé's stepmother to any of the wedding festivities. She's asking you to act in an unbecoming manner and to ostracize someone with whom you will have to interact for years to come. You may never be close to your fiancé's stepmother, but she will interact with your future children, and you certainly can't raise your children to disrespect their grandfather's partner. Your mom needs to understand that there is a much larger story to all this than "I don't like her; you can't invite her." With that in mind, it's time for Mom to bite her tongue and allow the two women in question to deal with the problem all by themselves. Hopefully, they will all see that the event is not about them and graciously support their children on their special day.

If Mom absolutely cannot get past her anger over this situation, and you fear she will make a scene, you may want to forgo the rehearsal dinner and just have a quiet get-together with the best man and maid or matron of honor. Thank the father of the groom for his generosity, but explain that you have decided not to have a formal dinner after the rehearsal.

> *"My mother and father are both hosting my wedding, because they both love me, but they have not spoken to each other in years, and I dread them being together at the rehearsal dinner."*

Keeping your divorced parents apart and fearing whether or not they will act civilly in public should not be your burden to carry. If time has not helped to heal the relationship between feuding parents, it is up to the adult child to release the responsibility from his or her shoulders and expect the parents to step up to the plate. It is their job to keep the peace, not their child's. Do not be afraid to politely tell them so.

Children of divorce may feel as if they had to run defense to protect one parent (or each of them) from the anger or sarcasm of the other—as if they had the ability to stop Mom and Dad's poor behavior. They didn't, and they don't now. Bad behavior was always the parents' choice.

Do not seat feuding parents near each other at the rehearsal dinner. Use other family members as buffers. It may be helpful to seat one at one end of the table and another at the other end of the table. If divorced parents are ill-behaved at the rehearsal dinner, it would not be bad ex-etiquette if someone from the wedding party—or even the minister, if he or she is attending—asks them to be civil to one another, and if they cannot, suggests that they both leave the dinner.

9

The Ceremony

The wedding ceremony is the ultimate public expression of a couple's desire to come together and create a family. This expression of unity can be particularly meaningful if the parents of the bride and/or groom are divorced, or if the couple themselves have children either together or from a previous relationship.

The wedding of a bride or groom whose parents are divorced or separated is handled just as any first wedding would be, with a few special considerations. Seating, in particular, becomes a problem if relationships are strained. Things get even more convoluted when both the bride and the groom's parents are divorced. This is where practicing good ex-etiquette really comes into play.

Encore wedding ceremonies can be more complicated than first marriage ceremonies, because they involve so many people with highly charged emotional attachments to one another. Using the rules of good ex-etiquette will help here, also, to make the day the loving, peaceful time all truly want it to be.

Seating When Your Parents Are Divorced

At a conventional first wedding, the bride's relatives sit on the left as you face the front of the wedding site. The groom's relatives sit on the right. (Unless it's an Orthodox Jewish wedding, in which case the sides are reversed.) The parents of the bride and groom sit in the first pew or row on the corresponding side. As the guests enter, the ushers ask on whose side they would like to be seated. If ushers are not used, people seat themselves. Life is easy, right? Then parents divorce, remarry, and perhaps divorce again, and the seating arrangements get vastly more complicated.

Children of divorce can have lots of people to consider: stepmothers, stepfathers, stepaunts, ex-uncles, etc. Where the heck do you seat everyone to keep disaster to a minimum? Just remember that the first three or four rows are set aside for family and honored guests. That means you can get creative with the seating in those rows, depending on how well everyone gets along. If all other guests are seating themselves, make sure it is clear that the first four rows are reserved.

Standard practice dictates that when parents are divorced, the mother of the bride or groom and her partner sit in the first row, either on the right or left side, depending on to whom they are related, and the father of the bride or groom sits in the second row with his partner. If the divorced parents get along, it is perfectly acceptable for both sets of parents/bonusparents to sit in the first pew. If the parents don't get along, but you think they can be cordial during the ceremony, all may sit in the same row; however, you may want to position younger children between them (your siblings or half-siblings) to serve as a buffer. And if all the parental figures sit in the same row, everyone else gets to move up a row.

> "I am getting married in a few months. My parents are
> divorced—and they hate each other. My dad has remarried,
> but not my mother. To eliminate any potential for problems,

I just don't think my dad and his wife should sit right next to or behind my mother during the ceremony. What's another alternative?"

A divorced mom usually sits in the front row, alone or with her escort. Dad usually walks his daughter down the aisle and then sits next to his significant other in the second row, behind his ex-wife. If this is just plain too close for comfort, use grandparents or other close relatives as a buffer—seat them in the second row and put Dad and his wife in the third row. Then the seating would be:

front row: mother and escort
second row: grandparents or other close relatives
third row: father and wife/significant other/guest
fourth row: honored guests or other family members

Sometimes Dad and his wife even sit in the fourth row. This is done either when divorced parents absolutely cannot get along or there is bad blood between a past and present spouse. It is inappropriate to relegate a stepparent to the back of the room during a wedding ceremony purely because he or she is a stepparent. Of course, there may be extenuating circumstances that make back-of-the-room seating appropriate—for example, if an affair broke up the marriage only a short time ago. But if things are that bad, I question if it is appropriate for the new partner to attend the ceremony at all.

Using good ex-etiquette does not mean that feuding parents must talk to each other. It means that they should remain cordial in public and put the children first. Do not force estranged parents to interact at your wedding if they don't want to. If they want to stay on opposite sides of the church or wedding reception, that's their prerogative; it may be a blessing in disguise.

"The mother of the bride or groom always seems to be seated in the front row at the wedding ceremony. My fiancé was raised by his father. Although his mother was in his life, his dad was the one he lived with. After all that, it doesn't seem right that his father and bonusmom should be relegated to the second row."

You are right, and this situation is an exception to the rule. If the bride or groom was raised primarily by his or her father, then Dad and his guest should be in the front row, and Mom and her guest should sit behind him.

Honoring Stepparents and Other Bonusrelatives

"Although my stepparents will not be participating in the ceremony, I'd like to do something to demonstrate how important they are to me. Do you have any suggestions?"

If the bride or groom is particularly close to his or her bonusmom, he or she may want to include her in the formal seating. However, take care how it is done. The mother of the groom and the mother of the bride are the last to be seated, in that order, and it is their seating that signals that the wedding procession is about to start. As a result, formally seating bonusparents at this particular point in the ceremony will upset traditional seating protocol.

The easiest way to modify the ritual is to seat the bonusmom of the groom before the mother of the groom, and the bonusmom of the bride before the mother of the bride. I have seen the mother of the groom and mother of the bride seated, and then both of the bonusmoms seated, but this can be confusing for the guests. Unless they follow the wedding program very carefully, guests may wonder who those ladies are and to which family they belong. So I prefer the first suggestion. It follows tradition more closely—guests automatically know that the wedding is about to start after the mother of the bride is seated.

Other ways to honor bonusparents are to ask them to say something at the reception, for you to make a special toast to them at the reception, to include them in the father/daughter or mother/son dance, and to offer them a specially made corsage or boutonniere. Or, you may want to offer them a flower from your bouquet or give them a hug as you leave the ceremony.

One of the most touching ceremonies I attended was that of a dear friend's son who lived most of his life with his father and bonusmother. As the wedding music began, he, not an usher, walked his bonusmother down the aisle and brought her to her seat. He then went to his mother, walked her down the aisle, and brought her to her seat. It did take a little longer with all that running around while the wedding party waited at the altar, but the groom didn't care and wanted to handle it that way. That was his prerogative and perfectly acceptable. It was a beautiful sentiment that demonstrated love and respect to both his mother and his bonusmother.

"Is there anything special I should take into consideration if I choose to seat my bonusmom in the formal seating?"

Yes. While looking for a way to honor your bonusmom, you may inadvertently hurt the feelings of the mother of the bride or groom. Seating is symbolic during a wedding ceremony. Traditionally, the groom's parents are seated first, and then the bride's mother, which signals that the ceremony is about to start. Adding bonusmoms to the formal seating could upset some more traditional parents. If you add the groom's bonusmom to the formal seating, she would be the first to be seated. Normally, that honor goes to the mother of the groom. She may have been waiting for this day for years. With this in mind, it would be best to discuss your choice with the mother of the groom so that she is not surprised by your decision. Remember to use ex-etiquette rule number seven, "Use empathy when problem solving," and rule number eight, "Be honest and straightforward," while using tact and timing, of course, when discussing your choice.

When adding the bride's bonusmom to the formal ceremony seating, she would be seated before the mother of the bride. Again, to avoid any hurt or embarrassment, it would be best to discuss your decision to add your bonusmom to the formal seating with the mother of the bride in advance. And, if that is your final decision, remember to list your bonusmom's name in the wedding program, as people who do not know you well will wonder who she is.

> "*Over the years I have become quite close to my bonusgrand-parents, who live nearby. They are so great to me and have always treated me like part of their family. I would like them to sit closer to the front because they don't hear that well, but my grandparents, who live two states away, have always been a little jealous of my relationship with them. How do I handle this tastefully?*"

It's not uncommon to have lots of honored guests when relatives have divorced and remarried—and the last thing you want to cope with when you are walking down the aisle is worrying about hurting the feelings of someone you love. I have found that a good way to solve this sort of seating dilemma is to have a meeting with the ushers before the ceremony begins. Since the bride and groom and their senior attendants are probably preoccupied with ceremony preparations, this is an excellent task to assign to the father of the bride, or even the bride or groom's bonusparents, if they have them. (Bonusparents are always looking for ways to help with the ceremony.) Bring pictures along and simply explain to the ushers where you want the players to be seated. This need not be discussed with the people as they are seated; the ushers can simply direct them to their seat of importance.

As for the question of where bonusgrandparents should sit, when you have so many people who love you, you may have to reserve the first five rows, rather than the first four, for honored guests.

> *"Both of my parents are divorced and have remarried, and I have stepsiblings on both sides. We are all adults now, but we all grew up together and are very close. I would like my stepsiblings to sit in a place of importance, and together. Even though they are from two different families, I regard them all as my siblings. Where do they sit?"*

First, since you have such close feelings for your stepsiblings, why not take the opportunity to refer to them as your bonussiblings? Because your bonussiblings are now adults, and you want to seat them all together, my suggestion would be to seat them all behind your grandparents, who would normally be in the third row. Therefore, the seating for a wedding like this would be:

> front row: mother and husband/significant other/guest
> second row: father and wife/significant other/guest
> third row: grandparents and aunts and uncles
> fourth row: bonussiblings and/or honored guests

Where to Seat Ex-Relatives

> *"My ex-stepdad was married to my mom for sixteen years. He helped raise her kids and loved us as his own. I'm getting married and have invited him, but feel it that it would be best for him to sit toward the back so that my mom doesn't make a scene. But considering how close my ex-stepdad and I have been, should he be seated closer to the front of the church?"*

It is common for ex-relatives to sit a little farther back during the ceremony. You can't be faulted for anticipating that your mother might make a scene or for trying to protect your ex-stepdad. (You can see why we like the term "bonus" better than "step"—once a bonus, always a bonus. "Ex-stepfather" just seems like a double negative and is not indicative of how you feel about him.) And your bonusdad should hardly be offended; there was a time when ex-steprelatives would not have been invited at all. The fact that he is being included means that he did his job well, that you realize that, and that you love him for it. He really can't ask for more.

Seating When Bio and Bonus Don't Get Along

> *"My mom really hates my bonusmom, even though she and my dad have been married for almost twenty years. I don't want a scene to ruin my wedding, and my bonusmom is nervous about the whole thing too. Where should I seat my dad and bonusmom?"*

If your father is walking you down the aisle, he should do that and then sit with his wife, your bonusmom. Some etiquette experts suggest that the new wife may choose to avoid confrontation by sitting farther back by herself while the father of the bride remains in his designated row. I question whether the father of the bride would want to participate in something as special as his daughter's wedding while his wife sits alone in the back of the church or synagogue. And I don't think this seating arrangement makes a healthy statement about the institution of marriage to friends and family—especially on a day that celebrates a loving union between two people. However, if you want to keep your mom and bonusmom apart, insert a buffer row between them. Therefore, the optimal seating arrangement for this particular wedding would be:

> front row: mother and husband/significant other/guest
> second row: grandparents or other close relatives
> third row: father and wife/significant other/guest
> fourth row: honored guests or other family members

The Processional

Below are the traditional Protestant and Jewish wedding processionals. In this day and age, encore couples or couples with divorced parents often borrow from the traditional to create their own unique processional. The many variations and alterations to these processionals are discussed throughout this section.

The Protestant Processional

The traditional processional—the trip down the aisle—for a Protestant wedding service is as follows: The mothers of the groom, then the mothers of the bride, are seated after all guests are seated and immediately before the start of the processional music. Next, the officiant, groom, and best man enter by a side door and wait at the altar. Groomsmen may also enter by a side door, or they can escort the bridesmaids down the aisle. The bridesmaids enter one at a time, walk down the aisle to the front, and stand left of center. The flower girl and then the ring bearer enter from the rear and walk down the aisle. The flower girl stands with the bridesmaids; the ring bearer stands with the groomsmen. They are followed by the maid and/or matron of honor. The bride is then escorted by her father or other close male family member or friend.

For the recessional, the wedding party leaves in the reverse order from which they entered.

The Jewish Processional

In Jewish ceremonies, the rabbi and cantor lead the procession, and then the groomsmen walk down the aisle one at a time, followed by the groom, who is accompanied by both of his parents. The bridesmaids follow one at a time, then the maid of honor, ring bearer, and flower girl, followed by the bride, who is accompanied by both of her parents.

If the parents are divorced, it is still appropriate for the bride's or groom's parents to stand on either side of their child as they walk down the aisle. If the new spouse of the divorced parent finds this offensive, the mother and her spouse may walk the bride or groom halfway down the aisle, and then the father and his spouse can walk the bride or groom down the remaining half.

The bride and groom are married under a chuppah, or wedding canopy. Parents greet their child with a kiss and then enter the chuppah. The groom walks the bride into the chuppah, and the ceremony starts. Men stand on the left as you face the front of the wedding site, women on the right. Parents stand under the fringes of the chuppah on their child's side. Best man and maid of honor stand by the front pole of the chuppah on the appropriate side. Others usually fan out from that point.

The Encore Wedding Processional

For encore weddings the processional can be as traditional or as non-traditional as you would like. I have been to encore weddings that ran the gamut, from those that mimicked first weddings to a crazy hot-air-balloon wedding in which each attendant flew in his or her own balloon instead of walking down the aisle.

At the most touching encore wedding I have ever attended, the entire bonusfamily walked down the aisle of the church together. Each adult had one child from a previous relationship, and each held his or her own child's hand as they walked. The minister waited for them at the end of the aisle before they all walked up the three stairs to stand at the altar. The mother and father of both the bride and groom, who sat in the front row on their designated sides of the church, all rose, walked over and kissed their adult child on the cheek, then kissed their adult child's new partner on the cheek, then sat down as the ceremony began. The children then sat in the front row with their grandparents until they were asked to rise, walk up the three stairs to their parents and the minister, and light a candle with their parents as a symbol of unity. These rituals conveyed a feeling of cooperation and acceptance from every family member, from the immediate family to the extended family. It was lovely, and it continued throughout the ceremony and into their life together. The choice for the family to walk down the aisle together does not follow old-school etiquette rules, but the result was lovely and communicated exactly what this family wanted to say to their guests. According to good ex-etiquette, as long as your processional communicates love and cooperation, it is the right choice.

Honoring a Bonusparent During the Processional

"I was raised by my dad and my stepmother. They were divorced last year, and my father is dating someone else, but my ex-stepmother is certainly invited to my wedding. I would like to offer her some sort of special gesture at some point during the wedding, but I'm not sure how, or when. I'd like to do something that won't cause a lot of commotion and anger my dad, but, by the same token, this woman raised me, and I love her. Got any ideas?"

If you have ushers seating your guests, make sure they know who your bonusmom is and seat her in an aisle seat. Before you walk down the aisle to be married, make sure you are told in which aisle seat she is sitting. During the recessional, stop as you and your husband pass her, pull a flower from your bouquet, and give it to her. Then continue to walk up the aisle to the exit. It's a lovely gesture that will say "I love you" without too much fuss. This is also a lovely gesture to offer any bonusmom during the ceremony.

A nice gesture to a bonusdad is to make sure he sits near the aisle, then during the recessional stop and give him a gentle hug before you and the groom proceed up the aisle to the exit.

Who Walks the Bride Down the Aisle?

"I'm engaged to a wonderful man. Our wedding date is approaching soon. We're both excited about it; the problem is

I can't decide who should walk me down the aisle—my father, who wasn't a big part of my life growing up, although we have a good relationship now, or my ex-stepfather, who I feel deserves the honor. "

Traditionally, the walk down the aisle is reserved for the father of the bride; however, divorce and remarriage are now so prevalent that this question often plagues modern brides. A child who has been raised by a loving stepparent looks for ways to thank him for his dedication, and helping to escort the bride down the aisle is often seen as the answer. The bonusparent regards this as a huge compliment. The biological parent, believing that this honor is reserved for him, may not see things that way. To make the predicament a little more unorthodox than usual, this bride is having trouble choosing between her father and a man who is technically no longer related to her at all. Who should walk her down the aisle? I have seen this subject handled tastefully in four different ways. All four employ good ex-etiquette.

First, the father and the bonusfather stand on either side of the bride as they walk down the aisle. The bride's father is on her left side; her bonusfather is on her right. If the bride would like to perform an additional gesture to distinguish the father from the bonusfather, the bride may take her father's right arm as they walk.

Another approach is that the bonusfather walks the bride down the aisle to the row in which her father sits. The father rises, walks his daughter the rest of the way, and is the one to answer when the officiant asks, "Who gives this woman?"

A third possibility is for the father to walk the bride down the aisle to the row in which her bonusfather sits. The bonusfather rises and walks his bonusdaughter the rest of the way. This choice was made by a bride who was somewhat estranged from her father, but who wanted to include him in the wedding ceremony. She explained to us that her bonusfather had raised her, and she felt he was her father. That's why she opted for him to be the one to present her to the groom.

The fourth possibility may be the source of future conflicts, but it may be the only answer at times: the bride may choose only one to walk her down the aisle. The final decision always lies with the bride.

"Can you suggest any alternatives to the standard walking the bride down the aisle?"

There are, of course, brides who ask grandfathers or uncles to take on this honor. One bride recently explained that she decided to ask her grandfather to walk her down the aisle to stop the arguing between her parents. Evidently, her mother was irate that she had asked her dad, and not her stepfather, to walk her down the aisle. To keep the families calm, she asked her maternal grandfather to escort her down the aisle as her mother and stepfather waited for her on one side of the pulpit, and her father waited on the other.

One bride with both a father and bonusfather wrote and told me that for her walk down the aisle, she chose to have not a conventional church wedding, but an outdoor wedding on her church's grounds without a center aisle. She had all family and friends sit together, not separated into a "groom's side" and "bride's side." She walked in from the side with both fathers, one on each arm.

The bride and groom may also choose to walk down the aisle together. They could meet their parents, bonusparents, and attendants as they wait at the front of the room near the officiant. This works especially well when the couple have lived together before marriage. In this case, no one officially gives the bride away; she and the groom enter as a couple and then say their vows of marriage. The attendants exit first, followed by the bride and groom.

Another untraditional choice I have heard of was a bride whose single mother, after struggling for years to raise her daughter alone, walked her daughter down the aisle.

The next suggestion is an example of very poor ex-etiquette, and I mention it here only as a reference of what *not* to do. A bride was having difficulty deciding who should walk her down the aisle. Her father had been rather flaky at the beginning of her life, and she was raised predominantly by her bonusdad. Dad eventually saw the error of his ways and was making an attempt to mend fences. In a misguided attempt to make the choice fairly and equitably, she drew a line on a piece of paper, symbolizing her life from birth to today. Parallel to it, she drew another line illustrating the length of time she had had a relationship with her birth father. On the other side of her "lifeline," she drew a similar line representing how long her bonusdad had been there for her. She then pretended the center line—the lifeline—was the aisle of the church. Her birth father would walk her as far as his line extended on the piece of paper, and her bonusdad would then take her the rest of the way.

This sounds good in theory, but let's examine what this is really saying to the guests: "Dad was a flake for most of my life, but now he gets it, so I will only embarrass him for a portion of the way down the aisle." This dad made bad choices previously, but now he was attempting to make amends. For that he should be praised. Granted, the bonusdad may have been the primary provider and should be treated with great respect, but not at the expense of embarrassing her father in public. Wedding days are not the time to make such a statement—even in metaphor. It would be far more gracious to handle the walk down the aisle in one of the other ways suggested and deal with the past at another time.

Who Gives the Bride Away?

Just as tricky as the choice of who walks the bride down the aisle is the decision of who responds if you're having the officiant ask "Who gives this bride in marriage?" Tradition stipulates that the father replies "I do" or "Her mother and I do." If the father is not present and the bride wishes it, her bonusfather may answer the question. He may want to answer "We do" as a symbol of the joint effort it took to raise the bride to adulthood. If the mother of the bride walked her daughter down the aisle, then the mother would answer "I do." Alternatively, a mother and father may both answer "We do" together. I recently attended a wedding ceremony in which the bride's adoptive father lived with a male partner. His response to "Who gives this woman to be married?" was "My partner and I do."

If a bride has an older son or daughter whom she wants to give her away, he or she could walk his or her mother down the aisle and then stand next to her. Under these circumstances, it may be more appropriate for the officiant to change the line to "Who will support this marriage?" or "Who will support this union?"

At perhaps the sweetest bonusfamily wedding I have ever attended, the bride had three young children who had lost their father in an accident. All of them walked their mother down the aisle to greet a man whom they adored. He had helped to raise them for the last three years, and the children thought of him as "Dad." The minister said, "Who wants to be a family?" The mother, bonusfather, and all three kids replied, "We do!" in unison.

The way you handle this aspect of the ceremony and how you reply depends on what you all feel is important and what will make you and your children comfortable.

Special Considerations for Catholic Weddings

"Giving the bride away" is not part of the Catholic ceremony. In a Catholic ceremony the woman is never "given" in marriage. It is believed that a man and woman freely enter into the state of matrimony. Although the woman is escorted down the aisle, the priest does not say, "Who gives this woman?"

Also, the Catholic Church does not recognize civil divorce. This means that if someone of the Catholic faith wants to remarry after a civil divorce, he or she must ask the church for special permission, and the first marriage must be officially annulled by the church.

Although it is best to discuss this directly with a priest in order to get the proper direction, I can give you a quick overview of what an annulment is and why one would be granted.

Unlike a divorce decree, which states that a marriage that once existed no longer does, an annulment is a declaration by the Catholic Church that the previous union never had the innate strength that distinguishes marriage. An annulment does not deny the reality of the wedding or the experience of the individuals during married life, but rather states that dissolution of marriage can proceed because something was seriously defective when the bride and groom spoke their wedding vows.

There are a number of well-defined grounds for annulment within the Catholic Church, including ignorance about the nature of marriage, state of mind when the wedding ceremony was performed (e.g., clinical depression or mental illness), infidelity, or a refusal to have children.

Demonstrating Family Unity

More than a ceremony in which two people are united in matrimony, weddings today often combine two families through the union of two divorced parents. Some might think that combining two families through marriage is a modern concept, but many ancient cultures understood the importance of family acceptance and integrated the extended family into their wedding ceremony.

The *datar*, or salt ritual, is a lovely tradition observed by Hindu couples immediately after they marry. At the groom's home the bride picks up a handful of salt and places it in the hands of her husband. He passes it back into her hands without spilling any salt—this is done three times. The *datar* is then performed between the bride and all members of the groom's family to symbolize that just as salt blends in and gives taste to food, so must the bride blend in and become a part of her new family.

The Unity Candle

In Western culture, the use of a unity candle is probably the most common way to symbolize the combining of two families in today's marriage ceremony. The candle display is most often situated at the front of the wedding site, near where the officiant will stand to marry the couple. It consists of two taper candles on either side of a large center candle. After the processional, for a first-time wedding, the mothers of the bride and groom each light a taper candle in honor of their son or daughter. They return to their seats, and the tapers remain lit throughout the ceremony. After the vows and rings have been exchanged, the officiant explains to the guests the symbolism of the unity candle. He or she asks the bride and groom to take their "individual" lives, symbolized by the two individual taper candles, and together light the large center candle. Then the officiant recites a special poem, or the musicians sing a song—whatever the couple wishes to do to communicate the importance of the union to their guests.

There is quite a controversy surrounding whether or not to extinguish the individual tapers after the unity candle is lit. Some couples believe that putting out the individual flames is symbolic of each partner losing his or her individuality after marriage, while others believe extinguishing individual candles only shows their devotion to the commitment they've just made. Most officiants leave that decision up to the couple.

> *"I was at a first-time wedding in which the mother and father both lit the bride and groom's taper candle at the same time. It was a lovely gesture, and I'd love to have my mom and dad both light the candle at my wedding, but they are divorced, and my dad has remarried. I don't think my dad's wife would like that. Got any suggestions?"*

This question usually comes up when a new wife does not want her husband to appear in public with his former wife. Jealousy and insecurity are frequently at the root of very poor ex-etiquette. "*We* are married now," new wives have told me. "He has no business lighting that candle standing next to her." If your dad's wife chooses to act poorly, you may want to forgo the use of a unity candle in your wedding ceremony.

However, if you are determined to light a unity candle, fall back on protocol. Explain that the candle should be lit by whomever raised the child, not who is currently married to the parent of the child. If both Mom and Dad played an active part in your upbringing, then both of them can light the candle. New partners must remember that when parents light the taper candle, it is a symbolic acknowledgment of their mutual love for their child, not their mutual love for each other. Their place in the lighting is as a parent, not a former lover.

Another very simple way to address this problem is to add another candle to the unity candle display and have your parents light candles one after another. Your mother would light a candle first, and then step back to her place, allowing your father to step forward, light a candle, and then step back to his place. The bride or groom would then light the unity candle using Mom's taper and Dad's taper, each holding one in each hand to do the lighting.

"*Is it appropriate for bonusparents to participate in the lighting of a unity candle?*"

The issue isn't whether or not it is appropriate. The issue is whether the divorced parent can accept a blatant gesture by which the bride or groom acknowledges the bonusparent's place in his or her upbringing. Some biological parents might find the gesture insulting. If that is the case, but the bride or groom still wishes to honor his or her bonusparent in the candle lighting, this may be a perfect time to establish a new tradition. Add another candle to the display and invite stepparents to join in after the biological parents light their candle. The bonusparents stand next to their spouses as they join in the ceremony.

Lighting the unity candle symbolizes love, respect, and extended family unity. Use it as a tool to communicate that to your guests—not as just one more thing about which a dysfunctional family can argue.

Incorporating Children into the Ceremony

There are many age-appropriate ways that kids can participate in a wedding ceremony and demonstrate family unity. Very young children can be flower girls or ring bearers. Older children can be junior ushers or junior bridesmaids. My own bonusson was four at the time of my marriage to his father, and he was delighted that he was asked to be best man. Our wedding was very small, and there was very little for the best man to do, so it was fitting to ask a child to be the male honored attendant. We let him pick the color and the style of his tux. It was the smallest tux I had ever seen, but a tux all the same, and allowing him to pick it out made the occasion fun for him. Weddings are serious occasions, but kids are kids. Include them in the preparations and make them fun and interesting, and the kids will look forward to the wedding.

Here are some other ways to incorporate your children into the proceedings:

- Have them sit in the front row, and reference them during the ceremony.
- Allow older children to light a candle.
- Offer each child a flower from the bride's bouquet at some point during the ceremony.
- Allow them to read a favorite verse or simply talk about their expectations.
- Have them sing a song.
- Have them pass out programs, throw rice or birdseed, or blow bubbles (whichever the bride and groom choose to use).
- Have them oversee the guest book.

"I need help. My fiancé has a daughter to whom I am very close. It is very important to me that she be included in the wedding ceremony. I need advice for how to not only celebrate the union of her father and me but also recognize the union between her and myself. Any suggestions?"

What a lovely thought, and an important consideration for both bonusmoms and bonusdads! There are all sorts of things you can do during the ceremony—and afterward. In the ceremony, after the exchanging of rings, you can make a special gesture by kissing her on the cheek. You can exchange a unique keepsake, like a pendant that you both wear. (For boys, you could present a lapel pin during the ceremony.) You can read a poem to her or say some heartfelt words. You can sing her a song. I've seen a bonusmom and bonusdaughter exchange charm bracelets, and one bonusmom gave her bonusson a rare baseball card for his collection right after she exchanged rings with his dad. You can give a special toast at the reception. But most of all, you can tell your bonuskids that you will be there for them— and actually be there, not just in words, but in deeds—and that will both create and reinforce a bond between you.

"I am remarrying after the death of my wife four years ago. My children will say a short poem during the ceremony. When they are finished, should they continue to stand with my wife and me at the altar, or should they sit down?"

Quite a few couples now want their children to stand with them during the ceremony. This can be awkward if the children are very young and unable to stand still. In that case, it may be best that they sit in the front row with the bride or groom's parents or an honored guest until it is time to say their poem. They join you at the altar for the poem and then return to the front row with your parents.

If the children are older, ask them what they would like to do.

Kids Lighting the Unity Candle

The lighting of the unity candle takes on new meaning when two people with children marry. It is an excellent way to integrate the children into the ceremony. Rather than the mothers of the bride and groom lighting the taper candles, both sets of children may light them. The bride's children light their mother's candle on the right, and the groom's children light their father's candle on the left.

If only one of you has kids, it could work like this: the child (or children) is given a candle of his or her own and sits in the front row until the unity candle ceremony begins. The child (or children) then joins the bride and the groom at the unity candle site. The bride and groom take their lighted candle and together light the child's (or children's) candle. Then all light the large unity candle. Some even prefer this approach when both partners have children.

Exchanging Rings or Medallions

A lovely way to acknowledge the combining of two families is to have both parents and their children stand together during the ceremony and pledge their commitment to each other. Wedding rings are exchanged between the parents, while smaller rings, pins, or medallions are offered to the children as a gesture of family unity. Bonus Families now offers a full line of jewelry (see page 199) designed specifically for ceremonies that combine families.

The Sand Ceremony

Each family member holds a jar of their favorite color sand and, one at a time, says some special words as they add their sand to one larger glass container. Each colored layer of sand is unique, but together the colors make one beautiful sculpture. This symbolizes each family member's individuality and importance to the structure of the newly combined family. The larger container is sealed and kept as a family keepsake.

The Bonusfamily Bouquet

Each family member in the ceremony holds a flower (either a different color of the same variety of flower or a different flower altogether) and says something personal as they place their flower in a vase to create a family bouquet. The bouquet symbolizes family unity while celebrating each family member's unique personality.

Incorporating Adult Children into the Ceremony

Many parents of adult children assume that even though their children no longer live at home, they can combine their families with few problems. In reality, the opposite is often true. Adult children have had years to build an allegiance with their parents. When a parent dies or a divorce happens later in life, some adult children have a very difficult time accepting their father or mother's new choice. Therefore, asking an adult child to participate in your wedding by being involved in one of the rituals described here is an excellent way to demonstrate your respect for him or her and your desire for bonusfamily unity.

An Uninvited Guest

> *"I'm afraid my fiancé's ex will show up and ruin our wedding ceremony. She's threatening to."*

I suggest that you take a serious look at your fears. Are you *really* afraid that the ex will wait for the line "If anyone has any good reason why the couple should not be married, speak now or forever hold your peace," and yell, "I do! Stop!"? Then your groom will leave you standing at the altar as he exits with his ex?

OK, it might have happened in *The Graduate*, but in reality, unless the ex wants to embarrass herself in front of just about everyone she knows—ex-in-laws, her children—she's not going to do that. She may want to make your life miserable, however, and that's a red flag for one of the following larger issues:

1. Your fiancé has not established clear boundaries with her for their relationship after divorce.
2. Your fiancé has not made it clear to her how you will fit into her life.
3. You have not established a relationship with her, and, if she has children, she may be afraid of your influence on them. Start talking to her so you can all successfully co-parent.
4. Your husband left her to marry you. If that's the case, you have an uphill battle before you. She probably won't show up at your wedding, but she is secretly pleased that you think she might.

If you truly fear that someone will attempt to attend your wedding who might do you harm, then security should be put in place before the ceremony. Alert the best man that you may need his help, or hire a security guard for the day. Do not be afraid to call the authorities and take out a restraining order.

Should You Just Elope?

Eloping may be more convenient than planning a full-blown wedding—especially when you are faced with the stresses of extended family or friends not getting along because someone is divorced. But all too often when a couple elopes, it upsets someone—whether it is the mother of the bride or groom who has been waiting for years for her baby's wedding, or the children of the encore couple who feel as if their parent's eloping means he or she is choosing someone new over them. So, weigh the decision to elope very carefully. Although it may be easier on you, not including family members in your special day may extend your family's period of adjustment.

Of course the final decision always lies with the marrying couple. If you do choose to elope, a reception when you return that celebrates your new union can appease family members and clearly demonstrate your commitment to becoming a family.

10

The Reception

With all the legal and religious aspects of the wedding ceremony out of the way, the reception is supposed to be a time for the bride and groom to relax, kick their shoes off, and celebrate. But not so fast. Divorced family members may be on their best behavior during a solemn occasion like a wedding. They may be less inclined to mind their manners at the reception. In this chapter I discuss everything from finding just the right place to have that reception to receiving-line ex-etiquette. If Mom and Dad are divorced, do they stand next to each other when greeting the guests? Does it matter if they get along? And has the proper ex-etiquette been established for the first dance as a new bonusfamily? Keep reading. This chapter is packed with answers to all your ex-etiquette reception questions.

Finding a Reception Site

The reception site you choose is often determined by the type of wedding you have planned. If you are having a formal wedding in a church, then the reception will most likely be held in similarly formal surroundings, say, a country club or fancy hotel. If you have planned a more casual wedding at a friend's home, then the reception is usually held in the same place, and as a result, it has a more casual feeling. If you have employed a wedding planner, he or she has lists of places to hold a reception that will match the flavor of your wedding. If you don't have a wedding planner, and you don't know where to start, ask the receptionist at the site of your wedding ceremony where he or she suggests a reception be held. You are not the first person to get married at the site, and the receptionist has probably directed many others to potential reception sites nearby.

Encore weddings are usually smaller and less elaborate than first-time weddings. For the reception, think tasteful but elegant, or even quaint, for the best results. For example, if you marry at a bed and breakfast inn, the grounds are often large enough for an elegant backyard reception. If you marry in a smaller, quainter church or synagogue, the reception can be held at a favorite restaurant that serves specialties you like. And if you have a theme wedding, then there should be no guesswork about where to hold the reception. For example, an encore wedding at a ski resort would include a reception in the lodge. For an encore wedding on the beach in Hawaii, the reception could be held either at the hotel where your guests are staying or right there on the beach.

Organizing the Reception

Organization is the key to a successful wedding reception. Even if it's your second (or subsequent) time around, and you're having a very casual, informal wedding, you should still have some sort of plan as to how the reception will progress, to ensure that it's a gathering to remember. It will help if you enlist someone you can depend on to move things along. Of course, for a formal wedding, this is where an experienced wedding planner can be worth his or her weight in gold. But if the wedding and reception are small, and you didn't hire a planner, you can ask a close friend or relative who is not in the wedding party to serve as the primary reception organizer. Another way to keep the festivities moving along is to work out a formal agenda and ask the band leader or the DJ to serve as master of ceremonies. He or she can refer to the agenda and know when it's time to introduce the bride and groom as they enter, announce the cutting of the cake, and then proceed to the first dance.

Ex-Etiquette for Receiving Lines

A receiving line is a formal arrangement in which members of the wedding party stand and greet those attending the wedding. If you have a large number of guests, it is probably the easiest way to acknowledge them. For smaller weddings, under seventy-five people, it may be easier for you and your new spouse to just greet your guests as they enter the reception or go from table to table saying hello. But the truth is, whether you decide to have a receiving line is simply a matter of choice and completely up to you. If you choose to go forward with one, it is done either immediately after the wedding at the wedding site or at the beginning of the reception.

When parents are divorced or it's an encore wedding, deciding who will stand in the receiving line can get a little complicated. Don't be a stickler about protocol. The goal is to keep everyone comfortable and avoid public confrontations.

As a starting reference, traditional etiquette suggests the following order for the most formal receiving line:

Mother of the bride
Mother of the groom
Bride
Groom
Maid of honor
All of the bridesmaids

Traditionally, men do not stand in the receiving line, except for the groom. Child attendants, such as flower girls and ring bearers, also do not participate.

Today, however, many couples prefer a shorter receiving line with just themselves and both sets of parents. The order would be:

Mother of the bride
Father of the bride
Bride
Groom
Mother of the groom
Father of the groom

If any of the parents are divorced and relations are strained, then a simple switch in the order of the line would occur. The line would then look like this:

Mother of the bride
Father of the groom
Bride
Groom
Mother of the groom
Father of the bride

Or you could have a line that looks like this:

Mother of the bride
Bride
Father of the bride
Groom
Mother of the groom
Father of the groom

Here are a few dos and don'ts to help you form a receiving line that best suits your family:

- Don't position divorced parents next to each other. Place the bride, groom, an attendant, or even the officiant between them. Officiants make excellent buffers between feuding parents.
- Feel free to ask stepparents to join the receiving line if divorced parents do not object. If a stepparent joins the line, the order should be:

> Husband of mother of the bride
> Mother of the bride
> Bride
> Father of the bride
> Wife of father of the bride
> Etc.

Some people may question placing the husband of the mother of the bride at the beginning of the receiving line, but since you are deviating from traditional wedding etiquette simply by asking a bonusparent to join the line, you must establish new wedding etiquette.

If your situation is simply too complicated and potentially volatile, you have a few options. You could have a receiving line that doesn't include parents, or nix the receiving line altogether. Some alternatives to the receiving line include:

- Opt for visiting each table to greet your guests.
- Have the DJ announce each parent and bonusparent as they walk into the reception hall. For example, "The bride's mother, Jennifer Smith, and her husband, Ron." Then, "The bride's father, Michael Manning, and his wife, Lucy." Then continue with the groom's parents and/or stepparents.

- Have a parents' dance where the bride's parents and the groom's parents are all invited onto the dance floor. If one of the parents is single, that parent would dance with his or her escort or a close family friend or relative. The DJ who is serving as the master of ceremonies would then name everyone who is dancing and their relationship to the bride and groom.

"My parents are divorced, and my father has remarried. Although I am close to my mom, I am quite close to my bonusmom as well, and her name is listed along with my dad's, plus my mom's, as a host of my wedding. Shouldn't my bonusmom stand in the receiving line next to my dad if she's listed on the invitation?"

Who stands in the receiving line is not necessarily dependent upon whose name appears on the invitation. Even in "the good old days" when parents rarely divorced, traditional etiquette suggested that the mothers of the bride and groom stand in the receiving line without their husbands, even though the invitations listed "Mr. and Mrs." as hosts. Traditional etiquette also dictated that if a bride's father and stepmother hosted the wedding, then they stood in the receiving line; the bride's mother was presented simply as an honored guest. If neither the father nor the mother had remarried, then only the bride's mother stood in the line—unless the father was hosting the reception. In that case, the bride's mother would not stand in the line, the father would, and the godmother of the bride or another close female relative would receive in her place. When the groom's parents were divorced, the groom's mother still joined him in the line, and neither his father nor his stepfather joined her—which sure made things a lot easier.

So much for traditional etiquette. Today, everything is different, and you may just have to throw convention to the wind and create a receiving line that matches your family mix. The only thing that is a no-no in this particular case is that your father should not stand between his first and second wives. Place yourself, the officiant, or someone else of honor between your father and your mother.

"I know my dad and stepmother are hosting my wedding and reception, but my mom just can't afford it. I still want her in my receiving line."

Good ex-etiquette states that it is perfectly permissible to decide the order of your own receiving line, remembering that the final goal is always to make sure everyone is comfortable and avoid public confrontations. It's completely understandable that you want your mother near you in the receiving line. Hopefully, your father and stepmother will put their child/bonuschild first and will not take your request personally.

"My fiancé and I have both been married before, but we decided to have a rather formal wedding that we are paying for ourselves. Is a receiving line appropriate for us? And who stands in the encore wedding receiving line?"

The beauty of the encore wedding is that when it comes to all this wedding planning, the specifics are really up to you. If you are having a formal wedding and would like to have a receiving line, then of course you may. However, since most encore weddings are smaller than first-time weddings, it may be more convenient to greet your guests informally.

The receiving line at an encore wedding may also serve an additional purpose—it is a wonderful way to introduce the new bonusfamily to guests for the first time. Rather than the couple's parents and the bridal party receiving guests, the encore wedding receiving line may simply be the bride and groom and their combined children.

> *"This is my third and last marriage, and my fiancé's second and last marriage! My parents are quite elderly—my mom's in a wheelchair—and they have flown in from across the country to come to our wedding. I want to make sure I introduce them to all my friends. Even though they did not host my wedding, is it inappropriate to ask them to join my husband and me in a receiving line?"*

Even though your parents are not hosting the wedding, if you would like to use the receiving line as a way to introduce them to your other guests, then it is perfectly acceptable to ask your parents to join you in the line—especially in cases like yours. If your mother is in a wheelchair, rather than being wheeled around from guest to guest, she can just stay put in the line, and the guests can come to her.

A nice touch to get the party started, especially if the reception is more formal, is to have a waiter waiting at the end of the receiving line, with a glass of champagne for each guest.

Seating at the Reception

> *"My parents are divorced, and both have remarried. My fiancé's mother has never been married. How do we seat people at the parents' table?"*

Good ex-etiquette suggests that you not expect divorced parents and their new partners to all sit together unless they have been openly socializing well before the wedding. In our family, if Sharyl, my husband, and I did not sit together at the parents table, people would think there was something drastically wrong, but this is because we have been friendly for years. Most divorced parents do not interact well, and the stress of a child's wedding might add to their inability to communicate. For this reason, it would be advisable to set up separate parents' tables. For example, a father-of-the-bride's table would include relatives of the father of the bride and his new wife. A mother-of-the-bride's table would seat relatives of the mother of the bride and her new husband. Even though your fiancé's mother has never married, she may have an escort who would join her at a third table, along with relatives from the groom's family.

"I get along with my ex just fine, and my daughter has us both sitting at the same table at the reception. My ex won't mind, but my boyfriend will. How do I handle this?"

As mentioned above, you could talk to your daughter and request a separate table, but I must reiterate a very important point. New partners should not get in the middle of divorced parents' parenting. If you are like other divorced parents who get along, you have worked long and hard to put the animosity behind you. Interacting well together at a function as important as your child's wedding is the culmination of all that hard work. If your boyfriend is someone you really care for, prepare him for this new-school divorce lifestyle; don't keep him from it. If you do, you will, at some point, be forced to choose between your boyfriend and attending a family function. That's not good ex-etiquette.

Slowly ease your boyfriend into family functions. This means that if you have not been dating long, your daughter's wedding may not be the right place to introduce him to your family, and it would be better if you did not bring him.

"Both my fiancé and I have teenage children from previous marriages. We understand that teenagers do not like to sit with their parents; however, at an occasion like our wedding, should they be seated with us at the bridal table or at a separate teen table?"

To demonstrate family unity to both your children and your guests, seat your children, no matter their age or marital status, at the bridal table with your husband and you. Others who might be seated at the bridal table at an encore wedding are the best man and his guest and the matron of honor and her husband.

> *"I would like to seat my husband's daughter at the bridal table with us, but she has a three-year-old son who is a holy terror. Where else can she and her son sit that would be appropriate?"*

In my opinion, nowhere else. She should sit at the bridal table with her dad and you, along with her little holy terror. Anticipating his antics, you might want to bring along some special treats to keep him occupied—crayons and coloring books, pocket Tonka trucks, etc. You see, this holy terror is now your bonusgrandchild, so avoiding him or ignoring him will not help you assimilate into the family. If he's a holy terror, he's not shy, so when the music starts, channel some of that energy constructively and get him up dancing! It will, one, hopefully tucker him out a little, and two, ingratiate you to his mother, your new bonusdaughter, if she thinks you enjoy being with her son. Not to mention forging a great relationship with the little guy at an early age.

Toasting at the Reception

The first toast is typically made by the groom's best man after the meal. The maid or matron of honor may also offer a toast. The best toasts are simple and sweet, perhaps relating a memory of the first time the bride and groom met, or the first time the speaker realized they were in love. A humorous toast is always well accepted if it is tasteful and does not embarrass anyone. After the best man and maid of honor's toasts, the groom stands, thanks his friends for the kind words, and then toasts his new bride. After the groom finishes his toast, anyone is free to wish the new couple well by standing up and making his or her own toast.

The same toasts are made at the encore wedding as at the first-time wedding, but the groom adds one more toast, to his new bonus-family. The best bonusfamily toasts single out each family member and say something nice about him or her, then comment on the groom's hopes for their future life together as a family.

> *"I've asked my son to be my best man at my upcoming wedding, but he's only fourteen and has no idea how to make a toast at the reception. Is there someone else who can start the toasting off right?"*

This is one of the negatives associated with asking a child to be your best man. Along with the best man distinction come some important responsibilities, and if a child is too young to take on those responsibilities, then you will have to ask someone else to help.

You can handle your problem in one of two ways. You can begin by explaining the obligations associated with being best man to your son, and making sure he is up to the task. If he is, ask him to prepare a toast to the couple, just as you would expect of anyone you picked to be your best man. At fourteen, he'll gain good experience by accepting such an important responsibility, and you should look forward to a memorable toast. (Your son would toast with sparkling apple cider, of course.)

If your son is just too shy, and your father is still living, the boy's grandfather would be a good substitute or a strong shoulder on which to lean if your son needs a little prompting during the toast. (An uncle or close friend could also be of help.) Another approach would be for the grandfather to make the toast while referring to your son standing next to him.

Grandpa would say something like, "And along with Jimmy [his grandson], Michael's [the groom's] best man, I would like to congratulate . . ." and continue to say a few words. Then Jimmy could finish the toast by saying, "So let's lift our glasses to my dad and Michelle!" (Or "my dad and my new bonusmom!" or whatever Jimmy calls his father's new wife.)

> *"My father passed on when I was very young, and I was raised by my mother. She recently passed away. I did not make a very good choice for my first husband, and my mother was actually relieved when I got a divorce. She met my fiancé before she passed on and gave us her blessing. Is there some way I can acknowledge my deceased mother at my wedding?"*

It is perfectly acceptable to mention a parent or relative who has passed during a special toast at the reception. As I mentioned before, my husband gave a special toast to my deceased father at our wedding reception. My husband was a long-lost friend of mine from high school. He and my father had known each other for years and got along really well. My father's death was unexpected, and it was his passing that brought my husband and me together. My husband did not tell me he planned to make a toast to my dad, and his words were so touching it made me realize all over again why he was the right man for me. The toast simply acknowledged that he loved my dad and knew that we had his blessing, even though he could not be with us.

It is often customary for the bride and groom to exchange gifts after the ceremony. My husband couldn't have given me a better gift than this lovely toast in my father's name.

Cutting the Cake

The wedding cake is symbolic, the first food the husband and wife share together. Cutting it together symbolizes sharing their lives and taking care of each other through thick and thin. That's why I'm never sure why young couples feel compelled to mash cake into each other's faces as they share the first bite. Feeding your spouse is supposed to be symbolic of your love and care.

Some encore couples find the cake-cutting ceremony antiquated and would rather skip it. Just realize, however, that guests do *expect* to see you cut your cake, and it is a perfect time to again display bonusfamily unity at your reception. I suggest two wedding cake pictures: one of only the couple cutting their cake, and one with the entire bonusfamily, all hands joined together, cutting the cake. The bonusfamily cake-cutting picture can look a little silly, because sometimes when you put yours, mine, theirs, and ours in a picture, the grouping gets crazy, but it's what the picture is saying to family and friends that is important. "We are together. This is our new family, and this is the first morsel we will eat as a new bonusfamily."

The First Dance When Your Parents Are Divorced

The first dance at a wedding reception is always a sentimental and romantic time. First the bride and groom look lovingly into each other's eyes as they dance to the rhythm of their favorite song. And then the problems start. That's when I get letters like the one below. It is only one of the hundreds I have received that describe the stress of being a child of divorced parents on your wedding day.

> *"My parents divorced when I was a baby, and my mom raised me as a single parent. Rather than the traditional father-daughter dance, would it be appropriate for me to have the traditional first dance with my mother?"*

Your dance with your parent is a symbol of moving on from your family of origin to create your own family. It is a time when parent and child can give each other one last hug, acknowledging the past while celebrating what the future holds. If your mom was the one who raised you, if you desire, it is more than fitting to dance the first dance with her.

> *"I was raised by my mom and my bonusdad. Although my dad has been in my life, my bonusdad is the one I feel closest to. When it comes to the father-daughter dance, is it completely inappropriate to dance with my bonusdad first? I've been agonizing about this for months. I'm afraid if I do, I will hurt my dad's feelings, but if the dance is symbolic, my bonusdad is the one I should dance with first. What do I do?"*

You decide with whom you can be the most honest, you explain your decision, and then you follow through.

A little insight for bonuskids in this predicament: bonusparents spend their lives sharing the children they love. It will not be a shock to your bonusdad if you bring up the subject. Therefore, I would suggest that you take your bonusdad into your confidence. Explain that you will dance with your biological father first, then him—that this is protocol and is not indicative of the place he holds in your heart. You may also want to figure out a special gesture to offer your bonusdad during the ceremony—perhaps a special hug or a flower from your bouquet.

> *"I would like special dances with my dad, my bonusdad, and my new father-in-law, and my husband would like special dances with his mom, his bonusmom, and my mother. What do you think?"*

Although a beautiful sentiment, that's six special dances, and you will have your guests waiting for about fifteen minutes as you shuffle around the floor with all your new family members. Normally, to cut time to a minimum, Dad cuts in on the bride and groom's first dance, and sometimes as a real treat, Grandpa also cuts in. But if your bonusdad cuts in on the father-daughter dance, that doesn't send the proper message to your parents or your guests. When it comes to dances with parents and stepparents, ask the master of ceremonies to prepare shorter versions of a favorite song, but dance to completion. Dance with biological parents first, unless you feel it is important to make a statement of preference—but be careful, this is a place where it can be easy to offend both bio and bonus. That's why it may once again be a better choice to simply rely on old-fashioned protocol—dance with bioparents first—and use that as the reason for your decision. Then dance with bonusparents if you are so inclined. For dances with new in-laws, integrate those into the dance mix as all your guests dance. You may want to alert the photographer so that he or she can snap a special picture, but don't make your guests sit through special dances with everyone who means something to you.

The First Dance When It's an Encore Reception

An encore wedding is usually a less formal affair, so the process of moving through the reception from eating to toasting, to cake cutting, to dancing may not have to be as orchestrated as for first-time wedding receptions. It really depends on how formal the wedding is, where it is held, and how many people attend.

If it is a smaller, more intimate wedding and reception, that first dance, again, is for the bride and groom, but a nice touch for the second dance is that the kids join them on the dance floor for a bonusfamily dance. Then, while the bonusfamily dance is going on, the bride and groom motion to the rest of their extended family to join them, and then their friends join in. Of course, first dances with fathers and mothers are perfectly acceptable; just remember that when a bride or groom gets married for the second or subsequent time, there are more than two people coming together in holy matrimony—

there are two families coming together. First dances at the encore wedding take on special meaning. Right from the beginning, your dance card is quite full.

Tossing the Bouquet and Garter

The tradition of tossing the bouquet is said to have begun in fourteenth-century England. (But so much legend and lore is speculated to have begun in merry old England that I never know if the stories are really true.) It is said that women of the day, envious of the bride's good fortune, tried to rip off pieces of the bride's dress, hoping that some of that good luck would rub off on them. To escape the crowd, the bride would toss her bouquet as a diversion. Today the bouquet is tossed to single women with the hope that whoever catches it will be the next to marry.

Throwing the garter began in a similar fashion and probably around the same time. Again, either legend or history suggests that the bride would throw the garter to the guests at the wedding, and whoever caught it could expect good luck. Today the groom traditionally removes the garter from the bride's leg and throws it to the unmarried men. The man who catches it is thought to be the next to marry. It is customary for those who catch the bouquet and garter to have a photograph taken with the bride and groom.

Tossing the bridal bouquet and garter are standard events for a first wedding, but not necessarily for the encore bride and groom. The encore couple have either done it before or may feel a little silly going through the motions with their children looking on.

As an encore bride, if you want to toss your bouquet, that's fine, but many forgo the garter toss. An alternative to tossing the bouquet might be simply asking the master of ceremonies to play a song that pays tribute to a life of commitment and caring—for example, "After All" by Peter Cetera and Cher or "Forever and for Always" by Shania Twain. Then invite all couples to dance as the song plays. The master of ceremonies begins by asking the couples who have been together less than five years to leave the dance floor. Then ten years, then fifteen, until the last couple dancing has been together the longest. That's the couple who receives the bouquet.

Socializing at the Reception

"My wife's former husband is deceased, but she remains close to her ex-in-laws because they are her children's grandparents. We invited them to our wedding, but I have no idea what to say to them at the reception."

Making small talk with people who share a past with your new spouse is indeed difficult, but not impossible. Take a deep breath and begin. The first rule in this case is, no matter how nervous or uncomfortable you are, make no comparisons or references to their deceased son, no matter what you think they must be thinking. Just thank them for coming and tell them that you look forward to getting to know them. It will help if you can say something positive about their grandchildren—"It is such a privilege to know Susie and Johnny. I know you must be very proud of them."

Gifts

For larger weddings, first or encore, many couples use a registry, either online or through the store of their choice, to let those attending the wedding know what is needed or desired as a wedding present. If the wedding is smaller, fear of being rude or presumptuous often prevents couples from telling their guests what they want or need. In that case, a gift certificate from the bride and groom's favorite store is a good gift option, or the maid of honor may make suggestions.

Sometimes guests bring their wedding gifts to the reception, rather than sending them beforehand, so a table should be set aside so that the guests can place gifts there as they enter the reception. Some guests will give the bride and groom money. The bride can accept the envelope in the reception line and carry it in a small, elegant purse. Alternatively, some couples place a decorated box on the gift table into which guests can just slip their envelopes.

Gift Suggestions for Encore Marriages

Encore wedding gifts are very similar to the gifts you offer at the encore bridal shower. I always look for things couples wouldn't buy for themselves but would really like and use on special occasions. Things like a nice picnic basket set with plates and utensils for a quick getaway. Or if the couple like sports, a sports blanket to cuddle up under at games—with both of their names and their wedding date embroidered in the corner. My close friends know I love photography, and they often ask me to take their family portraits. For a wedding gift, I look for a really great frame that matches their home decor or purchase a specially engraved frame. Rather than a picture, I place in it an IOU for a bonusfamily portrait. Then I snap a casual shot of the family before or during the wedding festivities. I have been known to herd the encore couple/bonusfamily into a well-lit spot for a family portrait to place in the frame.

When an encore couple has kids, it's important to consider those kids when planning your gift. Acknowledge them by either offering each child a small token of your best wishes or offering the new bonusfamily a present that can be enjoyed by the entire family, not just the couple. For example, give them a gift certificate for a family night at the movies or a family dinner. Or construct a bonusfamily gift basket with small tokens symbolizing things each family member likes; this celebrates the combining of personalities while calling attention to every new family member's individuality.

If you are looking to give separate gifts, perhaps one to the couple and one to new bonussiblings, a good gift for the kids is a game or activity they can play together. Board games are always a good choice. Include a card that explains your intention to offer a present that the siblings can play with together. Or construct a gift basket just for the kids.

"No Gifts, Please"

> *"Both my fiancé and I have been married before, and we plan to have a small wedding with just family and then go on a month-long honeymoon in Europe. When we return we would like to have a reception for friends—but we don't want gifts. The truth is, we are quite well off, and receiving gifts just seems out of place to us. We want the feeling of a reception, with a wedding cake and dancing. I have heard that it is tacky to include the phrase 'No gifts, please' on the invitations. How else do you say it?"*

Traditional etiquette dictates that you should never include a "No gifts, please" directive on your invitation. The reasoning is that although you are trying to be gracious, some people find the request insulting or they may be offended at receiving a directive that cuts short their good intentions. They may not feel comfortable going to a party or even someone's home without bringing a gift of some sort. These people will not be stopped by a simple notification on an invitation. They *want* to bring a present, and they want you to be happy about it.

The best way to approach this is to just let your guests be gracious. If they bring a gift, they are doing what comes naturally. If someone asks you personally if gifts are appropriate, simply tell them how you feel: "We desire only the pleasure of your company."

If you are really a stickler about the gift issue, while you're away, delegate a close friend or adult child to keep records of those who plan to attend and ask guests to respond by phone. When guests call and ask if they should bring gifts, instruct your representative to say something like, "No, the pleasure of your company is all they want." Know that no matter how careful you are to let your friends know that you do not want them to bring a gift—even if you choose to formally discourage it on the invitation—some will anyway. If that happens, just say, "Thank you."

Money Dance

"Is a money dance appropriate for encore couples or for couples who have lived together for years before they decide to wed?"

First, for those who do not know what a money dance is, the bride, sometimes along with the groom, dances with the guests during a specified song, and those who dance with her pin bills (or small envelopes with bills enclosed) onto her clothes. The money is intended to be used on the honeymoon or to pay for any unforeseen expenses that might creep up in the first few months of marriage.

The money dance is a tradition designed for first-time married couples who are just starting out. If you have been living together for years, technically, you are not "just starting out." Some younger first timers live together for a short time before they marry. In these cases, a money dance may still be appropriate. However, a money dance would not be appropriate for encore couples, or even for first timers who have lived together for years, who own a home together, or who are well established financially.

11

Destination and Theme Weddings, Honeymoons, and Familymoons

More and more first-time and encore couples weigh the cost of the "white wedding" and reception and feel that a trip to an exotic location with just family and a few of their closest friends better suits their lifestyle. Others find it impossible to deal with dueling family members and hope that a wedding out of town in an exotic, romantic place will be enough of a distraction that everyone will just calm down—and enough of an excuse for those who feel uncomfortable attending to graciously decline the invitation. ("I'm sorry, I just can't get the time off" is a much more polite way to say you will not be in attendance than admitting you're not going because you don't want to talk to an ex-relative.)

Destination Weddings

With a destination wedding, the ceremony, reception, and honeymoon, along with other wedding activities designed to bring the guests together, all occur over a specific period of time at a festive destination.

For example, if the wedding destination is Lake Tahoe in the winter, a day of skiing or snowboarding might be scheduled for the guests. The couple marries, the reception follows, and then the guests return home while the couple stays on for a ski vacation. If the wedding is held in Hawaii, a day of snorkeling or horseback riding on the beach might be scheduled for the day before or after the wedding. The guests return home and the couple begins the honeymoon.

As far as choosing a resort, don't trust pictures. You can hide a wealth of problems in photographs simply by choosing a different lens or shooting from a particular angle. Always check the facility yourself to decide if it's what you want. That means you must travel to the place you are considering well in advance and check it out for yourself. You may want to ask the following questions:

- May you bring your own officiant, or will they make some suggestions for people you can interview to perform the ceremony?

- May you also have the reception there? If so, do they have catering facilities on the premises? May you sample the menu?
- May you bring your own photographer, or will they suggest, or even supply, one? If they are suggesting a photographer, may you view his or her portfolio?

Couples planning a destination wedding without the help of a consultant can work with the resort's concierge, wedding planner, or banquet planner. Remember to call an area's tourist office to learn the legal requirements for marrying at the destination. For example, if you choose Jamaica as your wedding destination, most Caribbean islands require a three-day residency prior to the ceremony, proof of citizenship, the completion of several documents, and a nominal fee.

Couples who plan to cruise to a favorite destination can have the best of both worlds. Not only do they have the added ambiance of sailing to an exotic location, but they can get off the ship to be married in a romantic setting—on a beach at sunset or maybe at a quaint little chapel off the beaten path. For example, Holland America Cruise Line has its own private island in the Caribbean, known as Hawk's Cay, with a lovely little chapel for just such occasions.

"If we decide to have a wedding in a far-off location, who pays for what?"

The etiquette associated with a destination wedding depends on a few things. If this is a first-time wedding, Dad and/or Mom typically pick up the cost of the wedding and reception, plus the lodging expenses of the bridal party, but not their transportation costs. Just as you would not pay for the mileage of someone traveling to your in-town wedding, you are not required to pay for their transportation to an out-of-town wedding. If it is a couple's first wedding, but they are older, more settled, established in the world, or have been living together for some time, Mom and Dad may still help out with expenses, but that is their choice. It is not expected.

If it is an encore wedding, especially if the bride and groom have been living together, traditional etiquette suggests that they pick up the tab for the lodging, food, and beverages for the wedding day for their attendants, but, again, not their transportation costs.

If the budget is on the smaller side, you may ask the attendants to pay for their own accommodations as well, but they should be notified when they are asked to be attendants. This will enable them to consider the added expense should they accept your offer. If the attendants wish to stay past the day of the wedding, it is usually at their own expense.

As for the other guests, if the destination is particularly remote or expensive, it is not uncommon to reserve a block of rooms in the hotel where the wedding ceremony is to be held—but the guests are expected to pick up their own tabs. Good ex-etiquette suggests that all are told ahead of time that they will be responsible for their own lodging if they choose to attend. Another way to address a smaller budget is to have only immediate family attend the destination wedding and then have a more conventional reception once you return.

It's smart for a couple planning a destination wedding to negotiate a discounted rate for booking multiple rooms and to check with airlines to determine if group airfare rates are available. Some travel agencies specialize in destination weddings and have packages already assembled that will save you time and money.

Theme Weddings

Over the last few years, the popularity of theme weddings has grown by leaps and bounds, and it's easy to understand why. Choosing a particular theme for your wedding makes it a lot easier to plan. Just follow the theme all the way through, from attire to decorations. No wondering about what colors to use; the theme decides that for you.

Let's examine how you could use "winter" as the theme for your wedding. You will see how everything falls into place once you choose the theme:

Winter Wedding (November, December, January, February)
Colors: white, blue, gray or silver or gold
Flowers: lily, lilac, hyacinth, rose, chrysanthemum, carnation
Music: harp, strings, acoustic guitar
Location: anywhere there is snow
Decor: fireplaces, fur, wool wraps, velvet

The couple might also choose a Christmas holiday wedding:

Christmas Wedding
Colors: red, white, cream, black, green, Christmas plaid
Flowers: red, white, crème rose, baby's breath
Music: Christmas carols, choirs, Christmas love songs
Location: anyplace to do with snow—ski lodge, for example
Decor: fireplaces, Christmas trees, angels, wrapped packages,
   ornaments, mistletoe

If the couple chooses to have a fall wedding, their colors could be reminiscent of the changing of the seasons. For a spring wedding, pastel colors would be a natural choice. There are lots of choices for a summer wedding theme. If the bride and groom are avid water-skiers or they love to sail, their wedding colors may be reminiscent of the sea and shore. They may even want to marry on the beach, on a cruise, or on a large, chartered sailboat.

Honeymoon Registries

Honeymoon registries are a great alternative to traditional wedding registries, particularly for encore couples. For those of you who already have all the blenders, toasters, and coffeemakers you need, the latest trend is the gift of a honeymoon—that is, your guests can contribute to a portion of your honeymoon costs. A honeymoon registry is very similar to a traditional department store gift registry, except instead of registering for household items and linens, you can register for items to make your honeymoon a dream come true—things like your airfare, accommodations, activities, meals, spa treatments, dance lessons, etc.

You can register online with one of the many honeymoon registries on the Internet. They are easily found by typing in the key words "honeymoon registries." Be careful; there are quite a few. Register with only a reputable honeymoon registry, because you will be required to supply personal information. To determine whether they are reputable, find out how long they've been in operation, check with a travel agent to see if they have any knowledge of the registry you have chosen, and/or check with friends to see if any have used an online honeymoon registry and liked their choice. You will find some in the "Resources" section at the end of this book. Note that some honeymoon registries charge a membership fee, and some are free and sponsored by resorts or cruise ship lines.

After you register, be sure to notify your guests that you have done so, but don't expect all your guests to choose the honeymoon registry gift option. Some will be more comfortable buying a more tangible gift or giving cash, so it's probably safest to register for some traditional items, too.

Weddings and Honeymoons with Kids

Honeymoons originated in a more conventional time when couples married once, and if they did have premarital sex, it was kept on the down-low. Only a fraction lived together before marriage, and even fewer had children before marriage. Technically, the honeymoon was supposed to be the first time a couple spent time alone together as husband and wife.

What we previously thought of as a honeymoon may now just be another example of old-school marriage and divorce customs that no longer match our contemporary lifestyle. For first-time married couples, honeymoons are still a very special time, but they no longer carry the mystique of years ago. And although parents with children from previous relationships might like to approach that first trip after their trip to the altar in the same fashion as those in the past, because they have children they may not be able to have a conventional honeymoon. Who has custody of the kids may be the deciding factor.

Many couples spend a lot of time looking for inclusive vows and offering their children rings to symbolize family unity, and then jet off to be alone without the new family members they were so careful to include in the ceremony. When the kids live with the marrying partner full-time, according to the kids I've worked with, it registers, and many resent being pushed aside while Dad or Mom takes off for a vacation with a new spouse. If you are in this situation, one alternative to the conventional honeymoon, in which you go off together for a week or two of post-nuptial bliss right after the ceremony, is to go on a "mini-honeymoon" to start things out right. Take off for just a weekend and ask out-of-town family to stay at your home while you are gone. They can watch the kids and the dogs. Spend the weekend getting pampered together at a local spa and having romantic meals alone. Later, when the family has had more time to gel, that's when you can take off for that long honeymoon, just the two of you.

A conventional honeymoon may not have as great of an impact when the marrying partner does not have primary placement—the child might just go back home after the ceremony. But keep in mind that if the children are not scheduled to return to their home of primary placement right away, the honeymoon should be postponed until they are. That is usually only a couple of days, but it could be longer.

Or the couple can plan a "familymoon"—a wedding and vacation combination designed to build family memories and reinforce new family bonds. Many resorts have discovered the need for such packages, and they design wedding festivities around the extended bonus-family. With a little perseverance, you will be able to find complete wedding packages that include help with the ceremony and reception; lodging, extravagant dinners, and day and night activities; plus kids' programs and babysitting services. Check the "Resources" section at the back of this book for suggestions.

"It's Me or the Kids . . ."

> *"I have never been married and have no children. My fiancé has been married and has two children who live with their mother most of the time. We see the kids every other weekend and for most holidays. We chose a weekend when the kids are with us for the wedding, but this prevents us from leaving for our honeymoon right after the reception. I want to take the kids back early, but my fiancé says he wants to be with his kids until the next day, when he is normally scheduled to return them. On our wedding day? Is this a sign of things to come? Will I never come first?"*

Your feelings are understandable; you would like some privacy with your husband after your wedding ceremony. However—and I cannot emphasize this enough—the man you chose to marry has children, and the children have made a special trip to attend the wedding. You wouldn't invite friends to an out-of-town get-together and then leave them to their own devices once they arrived. You should treat the children with the same respect.

"Will I never come first?" is something secretly uttered by many a second husband or wife; however, no one wins when a new spouse puts him- or herself in competition with a partner's children. New partners must understand that it's all a cleverly choreographed dance to integrate kids from previous relationships, plus extended family and friends, all while building and maintaining a loving marriage. With all this in mind, a newly married couple may not have the luxury of taking off on a honeymoon immediately after the ceremony.

In fact, you may never have the kind of marriage you expected all your life. Unlike in a conventional first marriage, you started with children. Even if they aren't biologically yours, you are now a role model and a parental figure. Accepting these facts is the first step toward making an encore marriage last. Look for ways to integrate the children into your new life together. Make it easy for your husband to co-parent, and everyone's life will be more harmonious.

All that said, it is important to note that the primary relationship—the relationship between the two adults in the family—is the glue that keeps the bonusfamily thriving. If a father or mother marries for the second or subsequent time and continues to bond primarily with his or her children over his or her new partner, the relationship is doomed from the start.

Formalities

The need to follow the rules of good ex-etiquette extends past the wedding day. Once you're married, there are quite a few situations that demand special ex-etiquette consideration. From deciding whether to change your name to making uncomfortable introductions, relying on the rules of good ex-etiquette will simply make your life easier.

Names and Other Potentially Confusing Issues

Practicalities

If you plan to take your husband's last name when you marry or remarry, you'll need to notify and/or update the following records when you receive your marriage license in the mail:

- Social Security
- driver's license
- bank

- employer
- bills and loans
- post office
- passport
- your children's school

You may need the following documents to verify the change:

- old driver's license
- birth certificate
- marriage certificate

Important: be sure to book your honeymoon tickets in your maiden name, because your driver's license and passport won't be changed yet, and you will need them to match the tickets if you plan to travel to a foreign country.

Keeping Your Ex's Name

"I have kids with my ex-husband, and I'd like us to continue to share the same last name, even though I have remarried. Do I have to change my name?"

There is no law that states you must change your last name. It was done in years past more as a custom than out of necessity. If you want to keep your ex's last name so that it matches your children's, that is a decision only you can make.

Some mothers who worry about not having the same last name as their children keep their former last name and hyphenate it with their new last name. Therefore, if your ex-husband's last name is Smith, and your new husband's last name is Jones, your last name would be Smith-Jones. Your child's last name would remain Smith. The only one you might have to clear that one with is your new husband. Many men understand their wife's anxiety about not having a name that matches her children's, and have no problem with their wife hyphenating her last name. Others are not so accepting. Ultimately, you should make your decisions based on what is best for the children, not your or your husband's desires.

When You and Your Spouse's Ex Have the Same Last Name

"My husband of two years was previously married and has two kids—a son and a daughter. He shares custody with his ex-wife. Six months ago his ex-wife remarried, and she refuses to change her last name! She uses our last name, and it drives me crazy! Why would she want to continue to use her ex-husband's last name after she has remarried? I can't imagine that her new husband would agree to it."

There are a few reasons why someone may want to continue to use her ex's last name after she has remarried. First, as mentioned above, she may want to match her children's last name. Second, she may be well known in her field and have a reputation under her current name. Third, the name may be shorter or simpler. One woman told me her mother kept her third husband's name—Todd—for that reason, even though she is married to her fourth (and final!) husband. In this day and age, it's the woman's choice what name she will use.

Although some men are adamant about their wife changing her name to match theirs, others do not feel it is important. Because the law does not require a woman to change her name when she marries, couples are free to handle this decision in the way that best suits them.

One thing you and your husband's ex should know is that confusion often arises when former and new partners have the same last name. It is worse if you live in the same small town or school district, and both of you have to interact with many of the same people. Sometimes I hear from past and present partners who share the same first *and* last name, and the only difference is the middle initial. If there were financial troubles before or after the divorce, a name this similar can play havoc with your credit rating.

Sharyl and I have had our own name problems over the years. I often hear, "Pardon me, but which Mrs. Ford are you?" That can get quite annoying. Although I hyphenate my last name professionally, there are times I don't. Therefore, my name is Jann A. Ford. Sharyl's name while married to my husband was Sharyl A. Ford. To this day, seventeen years later, we still receive each other's bills, bank statements, and junk mail. To be honest, there was a time when it upset me. But I learned very quickly that you can either get upset about things like this each time you walk to the mailbox, or simply let it go. I chose to let it go. And thanks to Sharyl, I have received quite a few hefty discounts at various local merchants through the mail. Some I share them with her; others I don't. Don't tell her.

When There Is More than One Ex-Husband

When a woman divorces more than once, she has a few options. She can keep the most recent ex's name, even after she remarries; she can return to using her maiden name; or she can drop the most recent ex's name to take the name of a new spouse. As mentioned previously, some women keep their children's last name and hyphenate it with their current spouse's last name.

Changing Your Child's Last Name upon Remarriage

Some newly married mothers who opt to use their new husband's last name want to change their children's names to match their own. The reason given most often is family unity, but there are several things to consider.

First, any parent considering a name change for a child upon remarriage should know that unless the other parent has formally terminated his or her rights as a parent, you cannot legally change the name of a minor child without the full consent of *both* parents.

Second, family unity is about more than everyone sharing a last name. If the family is not unified in spirit, a name change will do little to help. In fact, attempting to change a child's name without considering his or her feelings may actually promote dissent within the ranks. If the child closely identifies with his or her father, suggesting a name change could actually extend the child's period of adjustment after your divorce and remarriage.

You must remember: unless your child's father has abandoned him or her, after divorce your child actually has two families—not just one. Promoting family unity by openly cooperating with the child's other parent will do more to help with his or her security and feeling of family unity than changing the child's name. For things this sensitive, it is always best to follow the child's lead. There may be times when the child initiates the name change, and that is the primary reason to consider a name change.

My own daughter asked to change her name to my husband's last name, and she wanted to do it in the name of family unity. She was the only person in the family with a different last name, and at the age of seven, that was a very big deal to her. One day, in second grade, she just started filling out her papers using the last name of Ford. The teacher did not question it, but my daughter's biological father did. He was not happy, especially because she is his parents' only grandchild and the only person to carry on his name. He allowed her to do it, however, because it was not a legal change; because he had no intention of giving up his parental rights (nor would I have ever asked him to); and most important, because he loved her and knew she was just trying to fit in. She continued to use the last name of Ford until she turned eighteen. At that point she began to use her legal last name—again, because it was her choice.

"Will it be a headache dealing with my child's school if we don't have the same last name?"

Schools are used to dealing with children who have a different last name from their parents, so there's no need to feel compelled to change a child's name for fear of confusion at school. There are some specific things you can do to keep confusion to a minimum.

Each year as your child changes teachers, write a letter introducing your child's primary caregivers. If you share custody, this would include the names, physical addresses, e-mail addresses, and phone numbers of both biological parents and bonusparents. Request two of everything, including notices about conferences, special events, and field trips. Finally, make sure everyone is listed on the child's contact cards.

Introducing Former Relatives

"I am remarrying, and many of my former relatives will attend the wedding. How do I introduce them?"

The trick is to consider to whom you are making the introduction and then use the proper explanation. For example, let's say you are divorced and are about to remarry. Your divorced son and his ex-wife remain on good terms, and both will be attending your wedding. You are having a conversation at the reception with your former daughter-in-law when someone else walks up to congratulate you. You might say, "Let me introduce Sharyl Jupe. She was married to my son, Larry." If Larry has remarried, you might add, "But now he is married to Jann Blackstone."

If the meeting is very casual, and you know you will never see the person again, you do not have to include a formal explanation of the person you are introducing. Use the same rules of introduction that you would use when introducing anyone: "Let me introduce Sharyl Jupe. Sharyl, this is Michael Smith." However, if you know that two people will meet again in a similar situation, choose a label in your introduction that will prevent additional embarrassing questions. In other words, rather than using the term "my ex-daughter-in-law," introduce her by the title that currently describes her and will not change—"my grandchildren's mother." This has a kinder, gentler ring to it.

There may be a time when you must introduce your ex. Again, this introduction might change, depending upon the context. For example, if Sharyl is at a casual get-together, she may say, "This is my ex-husband, Larry Ford." However, if she is at a parent-teacher conference and must introduce her ex to her daughter's teacher, a better choice to help put the teacher at ease and explain the relationship would be, "This is Melanie's father, Larry Ford."

> *"I was married to my husband for twenty-two years. We are now divorced, and he continues to introduce my children as his stepson and stepdaughter, even though he has been living for four years with the woman he left me for. Consequently, some people don't realize that we are divorced. Should he still be referring to my children as 'his'?"*

Legally, your children are no relation to your ex-husband after you divorce. Even after twenty-two years of marriage, they are regarded as his *former* stepchildren.

I feel compelled to mention that the tone of your question implies that you may be angry that your ex left you for someone else, and as a result, you don't want him to refer to your children as his. If your children are adults, it's up to them to make that call. If they are minors, then it is up to you, as their legal guardian, to say something—but be careful that you are not letting your anger about his infidelity cloud your judgment. This sounds a little like revenge, and if that is so, you may be hurting your children more than you hurt the ex. The deciding factors should be what your children want and what's in their best interest.

The situation you describe is one of the reasons I like the term "bonus." If you are regarded as a bonusparent, and you remain in contact with the kids after you and their parent divorce, then you can continue to call them your bonuskids. Otherwise, there really is no positive reference to the relationship. Being reduced to "former stepchild" seems like a double negative; it even seems cruel, if the love between bonusparent and bonuschild remains after the parents are no longer married.

Gossip and Embarrassing Situations

"At a party recently, I ran into an old friend I hadn't spoken to in years. During the course of conversation, someone brought up my recent wedding. My old friend looked at me and said, 'Well, how many times have you been married?' My husband was standing right next to me, and we were both embarrassed. I didn't know what to say."

I think quite a few people might have been tongue-tied at that moment. Your friend shouldn't have asked—especially in front of your husband. Your new husband probably knows your history, but your friend had no idea how you handled discussing your past with him, nor if you wanted to discuss such a sensitive topic in public, with the others listening in. To have it openly discussed in a crowd in front of him is in poor taste. In a private conversation with your friend, if you want to volunteer such information, that is up to you, but it should not be asked of you. That's just fuel for gossip.

If you are faced with insensitive friends who ask inappropriate questions, and you want to stop them dead in their tracks, simply respond with "Why do you ask?" That puts the burden back on them, and if they have been rude, it will be immediately obvious.

Getting Rid of Past Possessions and Memorabilia

"What do I do with family heirlooms from my previous marriage?"

When a couple divorces, family heirlooms should be returned to the family of origin, unless a pledge has been made to pass the heirloom on to a child produced from the union. Then an ex may keep the heirloom in a safe place until it is time to pass it on to the child. In my own case, my wedding ring from my first marriage was a family heirloom cherished by my ex-husband's family. It was made of gold that his great-grandfather hand-panned in the California Gold Rush. Four dates were engraved into the ring: the wedding dates of my ex-husband's great-grandparents; his grandparents; and his parents; and finally, the date we wed. Unfortunately, my ex and I were the only ones in his family to divorce, so there was a concern as to how to handle this precious keepsake. Out of respect for my ex's family, I returned the ring with the understanding that it would be passed on to our daughter when she married.

"Should you discard your personal belongings from your past marriage when you remarry someone else? Things like your old wedding album, your wedding ring, letters, and cards?"

That really depends on whether or not there were children produced from the union. If there are no children, as a rule of thumb, I always suggest you discard or give away memorabilia from the past to make way for new memories, especially if keeping these mementos makes your new spouse uncomfortable. Do some soul searching. If you feel as if you cannot part with old love letters, cards, and other memorabilia, it may be an indicator that there is unfinished business you should address before you marry someone else.

Concerning letters, private communications are written with the expectation that they will be kept private. When someone professes his or her love, devotion, or concern through a letter, he or she does so believing that the information will not be shared. Your breakup with the person who wrote the letters does not change that fact. If you choose to keep old letters, a special effort should be made to keep them private, in a place where they will not be found by a new love or children who may misunderstand the motivation for keeping them.

As for your old wedding ring, unless it was a family heirloom that should be returned or passed along to the next generation as previously discussed it is acceptable to wear it on your right hand if you want to and are single. But it is rare that a new partner will want to see you sporting your previous wedding ring, or any piece of expensive jewelry that he or she knows was given to you by a previous partner. It is best to have the stones reset into a new cocktail ring or pendant that you can wear without concern. I've also heard of people selling their wedding rings to pay for the extras associated with their remarriage. Honestly, a wedding rings is yours, and as long as you use good taste and don't advertise to the world where you got the money for your extras, it's your decision to do with your ring what you want—even sell it.

If you had children with your ex, then you may want to keep your old wedding album, love letters, and wedding ring for them. Sharyl had the diamond from her first wedding ring made into a lovely ring for her daughter. A wedding album could be the only pictures that a child has of his or her biological parents together, and that may be important to him or her. A wedding album also contains pictures of friends and relatives who may no longer be living. My favorite picture of my deceased mother-in-law happens to have been taken at my husband and Sharyl's wedding. To be honest, I have only seen a few pictures of the event, and that's enough for me, but I know my bonusdaughter cherishes each and every one. I also saved my wedding album from my marriage to my older daughter's father, and I gave it to her on her twenty-first birthday. She also has a few letters her father wrote to me around the time of her birth. I kept them, then gave them to her to do with as she sees fit.

So if your children want your old wedding album and letters from your ex, pass them on when you remarry. If they are still too young to make that decision, pack the mementos in an airtight container and put it away where it won't be found by mistake. Tell your partner of your plans and forget about the mementos until it's time to pass them on.

> *"I recently found my wife's wedding album and a video of her wedding to her first husband stored at the top of the closet we rarely use. I wasn't sure about what was on the video, and when I saw it, I was surprised that it was of them renewing their vows in a private ceremony. My wife's first husband was killed in a plane crash three years ago, and they had no children. I don't want her to keep that stuff. We are married now."*

It's understandable that you would prefer that your wife not keep these sorts of memorabilia, but after only three years, it's not that extraordinary that she would still have them. Your wife faced a huge loss not so long ago. Many people who face this sort of loss know that they must move on, but that process is done in stages. The last stage is to marry again and start life over, but it's not uncommon to backslide at times and revisit your anger or grief while still moving forward, or to hang onto things that you really should let go of.

You may view your wife's desire to keep her wedding album and video as proof that she is with you only because her first husband is no longer living. Don't go there. Feelings like that can only promote insecurity on your part and are certainly not conducive to making your marriage one that lasts. Neither of you can start your new life together with those concerns.

Rather than destroying the album and video, I suggest that she offer it to a relative, like her first husband's sister or brother, or maybe his parents or grandparents. It may be the only memento that her former in-laws have of their son's marriage. He had no children, and they will probably appreciate keeping a memory of when their son was young, happy, and looking toward the future. Be conscious of the fact that they may also want to stay in contact with your wife because she is the last remaining connection they have to their deceased son. This is nothing personal, nor is it an indicator that your wife prefers his parents to yours or her previous life to the one she has now. We, as human beings, have an infinite capacity to love. This is not an either/or situation.

Your recent marriage may have conjured up memories for your wife of her previous marriage. If so, that is completely understandable, but it might be time for her to seek counseling to help her work through those issues—and so should you if this is something that really eats at you. I have to say, the fact that you viewed the video in private makes me wonder if your insecurity about this subject isn't getting the best of you. That video could have been of a more intimate nature than a vow renewal, and then you would have been faced with the memory of intimate images of your wife and her first husband. If you want your relationship to work, you *both* must let the past go. It's the only way you will ever build a future together.

Finally, it's important to note that you found this album and video way up on the top shelf of a closet you rarely use. That may be an indicator of where your wife mentally categorizes this memorabilia—something in the back of her mind that she occasionally visits, but not part of her everyday life. You are.

Wills and Trusts

> *"My husband passed away years ago and left me quite a bit of money. I have decided to marry a man I have known for years, but he is not as financially settled as I am. I don't want my children to panic about their inheritance, which may affect their relationship with my new husband. How can I assure them that I have made financial provisions for them all, as well as my new husband, should I pass before him?"*

It's a good idea to address this issue early in your relationship, because it's not uncommon for stepfamily animosity to brew over misplaced money and inheritances. The current husband or wife usually inherits the estate, unless there has been a provision made in a prenuptial agreement, will, or trust. This means that if there is a piece of jewelry, a family home, or another family treasure that you want to pass on to a relative from a previous marriage (like your child), make sure it is designated in a will or trust while you are living; otherwise, the law dictates that your belongings will be passed on to your spouse.

It's best to take each person aside and tell him or her honestly of your plans. Make sure you tell your partner and all the children the same thing, or else you will be doing more harm than good. The goal is to ease what pain you can by making provisions ahead of time.

Resources

Helpful Organizations

Bonus Families
PO Box 1926
Discovery Bay, CA 94514
www.bonusfamilies.com

A nonprofit organization dedicated to peaceful coexistence between divorced or never-been-married parents and their new families. Extensive Web site contains helpful articles, information on support groups, and both face-to-face and online mediation.

Kids' Turn
1242 Market Street, 2nd Floor
San Francisco, CA 94102-4802
(415) 437-0700 or (800) 392-9239
E-mail: kidsturn@earthlink.net
www.kidsturn.org

Educational programs for families who are undergoing, or who have undergone, separation or divorce.

Parents Without Partners
1650 South Dixie Highway, Suite 510
Boca Raton, FL 33432
www.parentswithoutpartners.org
An international, nonprofit educational organization devoted to the interests of single parents and their children.

Books of Interest

Wedding Books

Bussen, Karen. *Simple Stunning Weddings: Designing and Creating Your Perfect Celebration*. New York: Stewart, Tabori and Chang, 2004.

Carlisle, Erica and Vanessa. *I Was My Mother's Bridesmaid*. Tulsa: Wildcat Canyon Press, 1999.

Cole, Harriette. *Jumping the Broom: The African American Wedding Planner*. New York: Henry Holt, 1995.

Cowie, Colin. *Weddings*. New York: Little, Brown, 1998.

McBride-Mellinger, Maria. *The Perfect Wedding Details: More Than 100 Ideas for Personalizing Your Wedding*. New York: HarperCollins, 2003.

———*The Perfect Wedding Reception: Stylish Ideas for Every Season*. New York: HarperCollins, 2000.

Munro, Eleanor, ed. *Wedding Readings: Centuries of Writing and Rituals on Love and Marriage*. New York: Penguin Group, 1989.

Nettleton, Pamela Hill. *Getting Married When It's Not Your First Time*. New York: Harper Paperbacks, 2001.

Norden, Mary. *Wedding Details*. New York: HarperCollins, 2000.

Roney, Carley. *The Knot Ultimate Wedding Planner: Worksheets, Checklists, Etiquette, Calendars, and Answers to Frequently Asked Questions*. New York: Broadway Books, 1999.

Stewart, Martha. *The Best of Martha Stewart Living Weddings*. New York: Clarkson Potter, 1999.

Self-Help Books to Aid in a Happy Marriage

Chapman, Gary. *The Five Love Languages: How to Express Heartfelt Commitment to Your Mate*. Chicago: Northfield Publishing, 1995.

Hendricks, Gay, and Kathlyn Hendricks. *Lasting Love: The 5 Secrets of Growing a Vital, Conscious Relationship*. Emmaus, PA: Rodale, 2004.

Hendrix, Harville. *Getting the Love You Want: A Guide for Couples*. New York: Henry Holt, 1988.

Smalley, Gary. *Love Is a Decision*. Nashville: W Publishing Group, 1989.

Wright, H. Norman. *Communication: Key to Your Marriage: A Practical Guide to Creating a Happy, Fulfilling Relationship*. Ventura, CA: Regal Books, 2000.

Books on Divorce and Stepfamilies for Adults

Bartell, Susan, and Joel D. Block. *Mommy or Daddy: Whose Side Am I On?* Avon, MA: Adams Media, 2002.

Blackstone-Ford, Jann, and Sharyl Jupe. *Ex-Etiquette for Parents: Good Behavior After a Divorce or Separation*. Chicago: Chicago Review Press, 2004.

Cohn, Lisa, and William Merkel. *One Family, Two Family, New Family*. Edmonton, Alberta, Canada: Riverwood Books, 2004.

Emery, Robert E. *The Truth About Children and Divorce*. New York: Penguin Group, 2004.

Lansky, Vicki. *Vicki Lansky's Divorce Book for Parents*. 3rd ed. Minnetonka, MN: Book Peddlers, 1996.

Neuman, M. Gary. *Helping Your Kids Cope with Divorce the Sandcastles Way*. New York: Times Books, 1998.

O'Connor, Anne. *The Truth About Stepfamilies: Real American Stepfamilies Speak Out About What Works and What Doesn't When Creating a Life Together*. New York: Marlowe, 2003.

Ricci, Isolini. *Mom's House, Dad's House: A Complete Guide for Parents Who Are Separated, Divorced, or Remarried.* New York: Fireside Press, 1997.

Warshak, Richard A. *Divorce Poison: Protecting the Parent-Child Bond from a Vindictive Ex.* New York: HarperCollins, 2001.

Wisdom, Susan, and Jennifer Green. *Stepcoupling: Creating and Sustaining a Strong Marriage in Today's Blended Family.* New York: Three Rivers Press, 2002.

Books on Divorce and Stepfamilies for Kids and Teens

Block, Joel D., and Susan Bartell. *Stepliving for Teens: Getting Along with Stepparents, Parents, and Siblings.* New York: Price Stern Sloan, 2001.

Brown, Marc Tolon, and Lauren Krasny Brown. *Dinosaurs Divorce: A Guide for Changing Families.* New York: Little, Brown Young Readers, 1986.

Ford, Melanie, Steven Ford, Annie Ford, and Jann Blackstone-Ford. *My Parents are Divorced, Too.* 2nd ed. Washington, DC: Magination Press, 2006.

Ransom, Jeanie Franz, and Kathryn Kunz Finney. *I Don't Want to Talk About It.* Washington, DC: Magination Press, 2000.

Web Sites of Interest

Divorce and Remarriage Sites

The CoMamas

www.comamas.com

Created by a stepmother and biological mother who share techniques for how they learned to get along.

Divorce Step

www.divorcestep.com

Provides consultation and direct services in the areas of divorce and stepfamily relationships.

Ex-Etiquette

www.exetiquette.com

Help from Jann Blackstone-Ford, M.A., and Sharyl Jupe on interacting with an ex.

Family Medallion

www.familymedallion.com

Jewelry and keepsakes designed specifically for the second marriage.

Second Wives Café

www.secondwivescafe.com

Articles, message boards, and other online resources for second wives and stepmothers.

The Second Wives Club

www.secondwivesclub.com

Online community serving stepmoms and second wives since 1997.

Smart Marriages

www.smartmarriages.com

The coalition for marriage, family, and couples education.

Step Carefully

www.stepcarefully.com

A Christian site that offers private stepfamily coaching, family mediation, workshop seminars, support groups, and other stepparenting resources.

Stepfamily Information

www.stepfamilyinfo.org

Nonprofit divorce, remarriage, and co-parenting help.

Stepfamily Network

www.stepfamily.net

The Stepfamily Network is a nonprofit organization dedicated to helping stepfamily members achieve harmony and mutual respect in their family lives through education and support.

Stepfamily Talk Radio

www.stepfamilytalkradio.com

Innovative radio programming for parents who are divorced, separated, or remarried, or who plan on combining families.

Wives of Widowers

www.wivesofwidowers.com

Online support for wives and soon-to-be wives of widowers.

Wedding Sites

I Do Take Two

www.idotaketwo.com

Guide to second weddings, second marriages, and vow renewals.

The Knot

www.theknot.com

Offers a gift registry, bridal gown search, local vendor directory, and wedding etiquette guide.

Modern Bride

www.brides.com

Complete wedding planning site for brides and grooms. Expert advice and local resources to help plan the wedding you've always wanted.

Things Remembered

www.thingsremembered.com

A retail store specializing in personalized engraved or embroidered gifts that are great for wedding attendants' gifts, wedding favors, and more.

Ultimate Wedding

www.ultimatewedding.com

Local products and services, wedding store, destination wedding guide, mailing lists, discussion board, poems, marriage license information, song library, and more.

The Wedding Channel

www.weddingchannel.com

One-stop shopping for wedding planning. Bridal registries, hotel and honeymoon accommodations, links, etc.

Wedding Details

www.weddingdetails.com

A complete wedding planning resource.

Wedding Solutions
www.weddingsolutions.com
  A comprehensive wedding planning site.

Destination Wedding, Honeymoon, Familymoon Sites

Atlantis Resort
www.atlantis.com
  Fine dining and beach club relaxation located at Paradise Island,
Bahamas.

Beaches Family Resort
www.beaches.com
  Luxury resorts in the Caribbean, designed for family vacations.

Carnival Cruise Lines
www.carnival.com
  Great rates on fabulous "Fun Ship" cruises to the Caribbean,
Mexico, Alaska, Hawaii, and more.

Celebrity Cruise Line
www.celebrity.com
  Voted one of the world's best cruise lines, by *Condé Nast Traveler*.

Clipper Cruise Line
www.clippercruise.com
  Small-ship cruise line.

Disney Cruise Line
disneycruise.disney.go.com
  A great choice for bonusfamilies with kids.

EverAfter Wedding

www.everafterwedding.com

Contains information on familymoon packages and more.

Experience Vacations

www.outdoorexperienceschools.com

Three- or five-day outdoor adventures back in time for the whole family. Experience dude ranch living, Native American living, mountain living, and more.

The Honeymoon

www.thehoneymoon.com

All-inclusive honeymoon vacation packages; information for destination weddings. Nationwide network of wedding and honeymoon specialists.

Honeymoons by Sunset

www.honeymoons-by-sunset.com/BestFamilyResorts.html

Honeymoon planning Web site featuring bridal registry and familymoon vacation packages.

Norwegian Cruise Line

www.ncl.com

Premium cruise line with itineraries worldwide. Site includes destinations, ships, news and press releases, and corporate overview.

Royal Caribbean International

www.royalcaribbean.com

Over 100 ports of call, including destinations in Alaska, Canada, New England, Europe, Mexico, Hawaii, the Caribbean, Bermuda, and the Bahamas.

Sylvan Dale Guest Ranch

www.sylvandale.com

A family-owned and -operated ranch that offers group events, weddings and receptions, and family vacations.

Honeymoon Registries

The Big Day

www.thebigday.com

Destination wedding planning site that features honeymoon packages and specials from around the world, as well as a bridal registry.

HoneyLuna.com

www.honeyluna.com

Honeymoon registry service since 1995. Wedding guests can easily find and purchase the perfect wedding gift online.

Honeymoon Wishes

www.honeymoonwishes.com

Honeymoon registry and honeymoon vacation packages.

Bibliography

Dubin, Julie Weingarden. *How to Plan an Elegant Second Wedding.* Roseville, CA: Prima Lifestyles, 2002.

Engel, Marjorie. *Weddings: A Family Affair.* 2nd ed. New York: Wilshire Publishers, 1997.

Jenkins, Jennifer. *The Everything Wedding Shower Book.* Avon, MA: Adams Media, 2000.

Post, Emily. *Second Weddings.* New York: Harper Perennial, 1991.

Post, Peggy. *Etiquette.* 16th ed. New York: HarperCollins, 1997.

Stoner, Katherine, and Shae Irving. *Prenuptial Agreements: How to Write a Fair and Lasting Contract.* Berkeley, CA: Nolo, 2004.

Woodham, Martha. *Wedding Etiquette for Divorced Families: Tasteful Advice for Planning a Beautiful Wedding.* New York: McGraw-Hill, 2001.

Index

adult children of divorce
  budget-setting considerations and, 40–50
  ceremony programs and, 69–70
  engagement announcements and, 20–21, 26–31
  ex-etiquette practice examples for, 12–19
  invitation wording considerations and, 107–116
  processionals and, 144–147
  rehearsal dinners and, 131
  seating-related considerations for, 135–137
announcements. *see* engagements and engagement announcements
annulments *vs.* divorce decrees, 149
Atlantis Resort, 206
attendants
  attire for, 82–87
  bonusfamily as, 74–80
  flower selection for, 61–63
  importance of, 72
  responsibilities of, 73–74
  selection of, 72–74
  as witnesses, 73
attire
  bonusparent, 86–87
  bride's, 82–85
  creativity and, 82, 86
  dress codes and, 82–84
  parent and stepparent, 85–87
  pregnancy and, 84–85

baby-bridal shower combinations, 125–126
bachelor/bachelorette parties, 126–129
bank notifications, 186–187
Beaches Family Resort, 206
best man selection considerations, 72–82
bibliographies, 209. *See also* book resources

Big brother parties, 126
The Big Day, 208
bill notifications, 186–187
blame *vs.* cooperation contexts, 7–8
Bonus Families, 199
bonusfamily
  as attendants, 74–80
  photography and videography considerations for, 65–66
  showers and, 119–122
bonusparents
  organizational and planning roles of, 51–71
  processionals and, 144–147
book resources
  bibliographies, 209
  divorce-related, 201–202
  self-help, 201
  stepfamily-related, 201–202
  wedding-related, 200
bouquet tossing, 172–173
bridal showers. *see* showers
bridesmaids, 72–82, 118–119
budget-setting considerations
  expense responsibilities, 42–50. *see also* expense responsibilities
  importance of, 39–40
  neutral ground and, 40–42
  photographer and videographer selection, 65
  planning questions, 39–40

cake cutting, 168–169
candles, unity, 150–152, 154
Carnival Cruise Lines, 206
Catholic-specific considerations, 148–149
Celebrity Cruise Line, 206
ceremonies
  Catholic-specific considerations for, 148–149
  children and, 152–155

eloping and, 156
family unity demonstrations and,
149–155. *see also* family unity
demonstrations
"giving away" considerations,
147–148
importance of, 134
processionals for, 142–147. *see also*
processionals
program selection and composition,
69–71
seating-related considerations for,
135–142. *see also* seating-related
considerations
security issues for, 156
uninvited guests and, 155–156
certificates, gift, 173–174. *see also* gifts
child name change considerations,
187–191
child-specific considerations
for ceremonies, 152–155
for engagement announcements, 25–28
familymoons, 182–185
for guest lists and invitations, 94–96
for vow selection, 59–61
Clipper Cruise Line, 206
co-officiants, 58
CoMamas, 202–203
combination showers, baby-bridal,
125–126
communication principles, effective. *see*
effective communication principles
cooperation *vs.* blame contexts, 7–8
couples showers, 124–125
cruise lines, 206–208

dances
first, 169–172
money, 176
datars/salt rituals, 149
date selection, 54–57
deceased parents, engagement announcements and, 31–32
destination weddings, 178–180, 206–208
Disney Cruise Line, 206
divorce-related resources, 201–205
Divorce Step, 203
dress codes, 82–84
driver's license issues, 186–187

effective communication principles
actions/behaviors for, 6–7
cooperation *vs.* blame contexts, 7–8
interactions, past *vs.* present, 11–12
mutual interest acknowledgments, 12
negative emotions impacts, 10–11

old communication patterns, breaking
of, 8–10
eloping, 156
embarrassing situations, 193–194
emotion impacts, negative, 10–11
engagements and engagement announcements
adult children and, 26–28
deceased parents and, 31–32
divorced parents and, 20–21, 29–31
engagement parties, 33–34
ex-spouses and, 21–25
extended family protocols for, 28
grieving periods and, 35
importance of, 20–21
newspaper announcements, 28–33
parent announcements, 32–33
pre-divorce, 35–36
prenuptial agreements and, 36–38
self-announcements, 32
timing of, 34–35
younger children and, 25–26
EverAfter Wedding, 207
ex-bonusparents
guest list and invitation considerations
for, 106–107
rehearsal dinners and, 131–132
Ex-Etiquette Web site, 203
ex-relatives
as attendants, 80–82
guest list and invitation considerations
for, 92–94
ex-spouses
effective communication with, 6–12
engagement announcements and,
21–24, 35–36
guest list and invitation considerations
for, 89–92
names, keeping of, 187–188
expense responsibilities. *see also* budget-
setting considerations
divorced parents and, 44–48
nontraditional, 48–50
traditional, 42–44
Experience Vacations, 207

Family Medallion, 203
family unity demonstrations
bonusfamily bouquet, 155
datars/salt rituals, 149
importance of, 149
sand ceremony, 154
unity candles, 150–152, 154
Familymoon-related Web sites, 206–208
familymoons, 182–185
first dances, 169–172

flower girls, 72–82
flower selection, 61–63
formalities
    embarrassing situations and, 193–194
    former relative introductions, 191–193
    gossip and, 193–194
    importance of, 186
    name-related, 186–191. *see also* name-related formalities
    past possessions and memorabilia, disposition of, 194–198
    wills and trusts, 198

games, shower, 123–124
garter tossing, 172–173
gifts
    for children, 174–175
    at engagement parties, 34
    gift baskets, 174–175
    gift certificates, 173–174
    money as, 174
    money dances, 176
    "no gifts, please" directives, 175–176
    pictures and picture frames as, 174
    at receptions, 173–174
    registries, 173
    shower, 122–123
    suggestions for, 174–175
"giving away" considerations, 57–58, 147–148
gossip-related issues, 193–194
grieving periods, 35
groomsmen/ushers, 72–82
groundwork laying considerations
    for adult children of divorce, 12–19
    effective communication principles, 6–12. *see also* effective communication principles
    importance of, 1–6
    ten rules of good ex-etiquette, 6
    theory *vs.* practice examples, 12–19
guest lists and invitations, 88–116
    absentee parents and, 102
    for adult children of divorce, 100–116
    for bachelor/bachelorette parties, 127–128. *see also* bachelor/bachelorette parties
    child-specific considerations for, 94–96
    ex-bonusparents and, 106–107
    ex-relatives and, 92–94
    ex-spouses and, 89–92
    importance of, 88
    "other man/woman" and, 102–106
    out-of-control lists, 101–102
    for rehearsal dinners, 130–131
    "save the date" cards, 55–57

for showers, 119–122
uninvited guests and, 155–156
wording of, 96–100, 107–116

holiday weddings, 181
Honey Wishes, 208
HoneyLuna, 208
The Honeymoon, 207
honeymoons
    vs. familymoons, 182–185
    name change-related considerations for, 187
    registries for, 181–182, 208
    Web sites for, 206–208
Honeymoons by Sunset, 207

I Do Take Two, 204
interactions, past *vs.* present, 11–12
internet resources. *see* Web sites
invitations and guest lists. *see* guest lists and invitations

Jewish processionals, 142–143. *see also* processionals
junior bridesmaids and groomsmen/ushers, 72–82

Kids' Turn, 199
The Knot, 205

lender, bill, and bank notifications, 186–187
lists, guest. *see* guest lists and invitations

maid/matron of honor, 72–82
mail delivery notifications, 187
memorabilia, disposition of, 194–198
Mini-honeymoons, 183
Modern Bride, 205
money
    dances, 176
    as gifts, 174
multiple ex-husbands, name-related issues, 189
music and soloist selection, 67–69
mutual interest acknowledgments, 12

name-related formalities. *see also* formalities
    bank, bill, and lender notifications, 186–187
    child name change considerations, 187–191
    driver's license issues and, 186–187
    ex-spouse names, keeping of, 187–188
    honeymoon travel plans and, 187
    multiple ex-husbands and, 189

passport-related issues, 187
post office notifications, 187
practicalities of, 186–187
school notifications, 187, 190–191
shared ex-spouse names and, 188–189
Social Security issues and, 186–187
negative emotion impacts, 10–11
newspaper announcements, 28–33
"no gifts, please" directives, 175–176. *see also* gifts
nontraditional scenarios
destination weddings, 178–180
familymoons, 182–185
honeymoon registries, 181–182
importance of, 177–178
theme weddings, 180–181
Norwegian Cruise Line, 207

officiant selection, 57–58
old communication patterns, breaking of, 8–10
organizational and planning considerations. *see* planning and organizational considerations
out-of-control guest lists, 101
out-of-town guests, 130–132

Parents Without Partners, 200
parties
bachelor/bachelorette, 126–129
engagement, 33–34
passport-related issues, 187
past possessions, disposition of, 194–198
photographer and videographer selection
bonusfamily positions and, 65–67
budget-cutting considerations for, 65
tips for, 64–65
planning and organizational considerations
budget-setting and, 40. *see also* budget-setting considerations
ceremony program selection and composition, 69–71
date selection, 54–57
decision-making participant selection, 51–52
flower selection, 61–63
importance of, 51–52
music and soloist selection, 67–69
officiant selection, 57–58
photographer and videographer selections and, 64–67
for receptions, 158–159
"save the date" cards, 55–57
site selection, 52–54
vow choices and selection, 58–61
post office notifications, 187

practice *vs.* theory examples, 12–19
pre-divorce engagement announcements, 35–36
pregnancy, attire-related considerations for, 84–85
preliminary ex-etiquette considerations for adult children of divorce, 12–19
effective communication principles, 6–12. *see also* effective communication principles
importance of, 1–6
ten rules of good ex-etiquette, 6
theory *vs.* practice examples, 12–19
prenuptial agreements, 36–38
present *vs.* past interactions, 11–12
processionals. *see also* ceremonies
bonusparents and, 144
Jewish, 142–143
Protestant, 142
traditional *vs.* nontraditional, 142–144
walking brides down the aisle, 147–148
Protestant processionals, 142

receiving lines, 159–164
receptions
bouquet tossing at, 172–173
cake cutting at, 168–169
first dances at, 169–172
garter tossing at, 172–173
gift-giving at, 173–176. *see also* gifts
importance of, 157
organization of, 158–159
receiving lines, 159–164
seating at, 164–166
site selection for, 157–158
socializing at, 172
success of, 158
toasting at, 166–168
registries
bridal, 125
gift, 173
honeymoon, 208
rehearsal dinners
children and, 131
divorced parents and, 131–133
formal *vs.* informal, 130
guest lists for, 130–132
importance of, 130
out-of-town guests and, 130–131
remarriage-related Web sites, 202–205
resources
book, 200–202, 209
honeymoon registries, 208
organization, 199–200
Web sites, 202–208

ring bearers, 72–82
Royal Caribbean International, 207

salt rituals/datars, 149
sand ceremony, 154
"save the date" cards, 55–57
school notifications, 187, 190–191
seating-related considerations
    for bonusrelatives, 137–141
    for ceremonies, 135–142
    for divorced parents, 135–137
    for ex-relatives, 140–141
    for receptions, 164–166
    for stepparents, 137–140
Second Wives Café, 203
security-related issues, 156
selection-related considerations. see plan-
    ning and organizational considera-
    tions
self-help book resources, 201
shared ex-spouse names, 188–189
showers
    baby-bridal combinations, 125–126
    bridal registries and, 125
    couples, 124–125
    games at, 123–124
    guest lists and invitations for, 119–122
    hosting of, 118–119
    importance of, 117–118
    number of, 124–125
    shower gifts, 122–123
site selection considerations
    for ceremonies, 52–54
    for receptions, 157–158
Smart Marriages, 203
Social Security issues, 186–187
socializing-related contexts, 172
soloist and music selection, 67–69
Step Carefully, 204
Stepfamily Information, 204
Stepfamily Network, 204
stepfamily-related book resources,
    201–202
Stepfamily Talk Radio, 204
Sylvan Dale Guest Ranch, 208

ten rules of good ex-etiquette, 5–6
theme weddings, 180–181

theory vs. practice examples, 12–19
Things Remembered, 205
time between marriages, 34–35
toasting, 166–168
tossing
    of bouquets, 172–173
    of garters, 172–173
trusts and wills, 198

Ultimate Wedding, 205
uninvited guests, 155–156
unity candles, 150–152, 154
unity demonstrations. see family unity
    demonstrations
ushers/groomsmen, 72–82

videographer and photographer selection
    bonusfamily positions and, 65–67
    budget-cutting considerations for, 65
    importance of, 64
    tips for, 64–65
vow choices and selection, 58–61

walking brides down the aisle, 147–148
weather-related considerations, 55
Web sites
    destination wedding-related, 206–208
    divorce-related, 202–205
    honeymoon- and familymoon-related,
        206–208
    of organizations, 199–200
    registries, honeymoon, 208
    remarriage-related, 202–205
    wedding-related, 204–206
wedding ceremonies. see ceremonies
The Wedding Channel, 205
Wedding Details, 206
wedding parties. see also attendants
    attire for, 82–87
    members of, 72–82
    traditional, 72
wedding resources. see resources
Wedding Solutions, 206
wills and trusts, 198
witnesses, 73
Wives of Widowers, 204
wording, invitations, 96–100, 107–116.
    see also guest lists and invitations